Holt McDougal

Geometry

Larson   Boswell   Kanold   Stiff

Practice Workbook

The Practice Workbook provides additional practice
for every lesson in the textbook. The workbook covers
essential vocabulary, skills, and problem solving. Space
is provided for students to show their work.

HOLT McDOUGAL

  HOUGHTON MIFFLIN HARCOURT

COMMON
CORE

EDITION

ISBN 978-0-547-71004-4

 4 5 6 7 8 9 10   0982   20 19 18 17 16 15 14

4500460631

Contents

Chapter

Contents

Name _____ Date _____

Use the diagram to decide whether the given statement is *true* or *false*.

1. Points *H*, *I*, and *G* are collinear.

2. Points *H*, *I*, and *J* are coplanar.

3. $\overrightarrow{EG}$ and $\overrightarrow{FG}$ are opposite rays.

4. All points on $\overleftrightarrow{GI}$ and $\overrightarrow{GF}$ are coplanar.

5. The intersection of $\overleftrightarrow{EF}$ and plane *JKH* is $\overleftrightarrow{HI}$.

6. The intersection of $\overleftrightarrow{EF}$, $\overleftrightarrow{HI}$, and $\overleftrightarrow{JG}$ is point *G*.

7. The intersection of plane *EGH* and plane *JGI* is point *G*.

8. The intersection of plane *EFI* and plane *JKG* is $\overleftrightarrow{HG}$.

Sketch the figure described.

9. Two rays that do not intersect

10. Three planes that intersect in one line

11. Three lines that intersect in three points

12. A ray that intersects a plane in one point

In Exercises 13–15, use the diagram.

13. Name 12 different rays.

14. Name a pair of opposite rays.

15. Name 3 lines that intersect at point *C*.

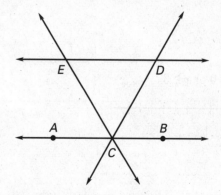

LESSON 1.1

Practice continued

For use with the lesson "Identify Points, Lines, and Planes"

16. Draw four noncollinear points A, B, C, and D. Then sketch $\overline{AB}$, $\overrightarrow{BC}$, and $\overleftrightarrow{AD}$.

17. Sketch plane M intersecting plane N. Then sketch plane O so that it intersects plane N, but not plane M.

You are given an equation of a line and a point. Use substitution to determine whether the point is on the line.

18. $y = 5x + 3$; $A(1, 8)$

19. $y = -x + 3$; $A(6, 3)$

20. $y = -3x - 6$; $A(2, 0)$

21. $2x - y = 7$; $A(3, -1)$

22. $x + 6y = 40$; $A(-10, 5)$

23. $-x - 4y = -14$; $A(-6, 2)$

Graph the inequality on a number line. Tell whether the graph is a *segment*, a *ray* or *rays*, a *point*, or a *line*.

24. $x \geq 2$

25. $2 \leq x \leq 5$

26. $x \leq 0$ or $x \geq 8$

27. $|x| \leq 0$

LESSON 1.1

Practice *continued*

For use with the lesson "Identify Points, Lines, and Planes"

28. Counter Stools Two different types of stools are shown below.

a. One stool rocks slightly from side to side on your kitchen floor. Which of the two stools could this possibly be? *Explain* why this might occur.

Three-legged stool   Four-legged stool

b. Suppose that each stool is placed on a flat surface that is slightly sloped. Do you expect either of the stools to rock from side to side? *Explain* why or why not.

29. Perspective Drawings Recall from the text, that a perspective drawing is drawn using vanishing points.

a. Does the drawing at the right represent a perspective drawing? *Explain* why or why not.

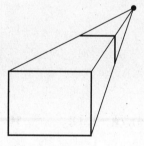

b. Using heavy dashed lines, draw the hidden lines of the prism.

c. Redraw the prism so that it uses two vanishing points.

Name _____ Date _____

Measure the length of the segment to the nearest tenth of a centimeter.

1. A ————————————— B

2. M ————— N

3. E ————————— F

Use the Segment Addition Postulate to find the indicated length.

4. Find *RT*.

    R ——17—— S —8.5— T

5. Find *BC*.

    |———— 54 ————|
    A   25   B   C

6. Find *MN*.

    |————— 32 —————|
    M   N   26   P

Plot the given points in a coordinate plane. Then determine whether the line segments named are congruent.

7. $A(2, 2), B(4, 2), C(-1, -1), D(-1, 1)$;

    $\overline{AB}$ and $\overline{CD}$

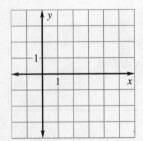

8. $M(1, -3), N(4, -3), O(3, 4), P(4, 4)$;

    $\overline{MN}$ and $\overline{OP}$

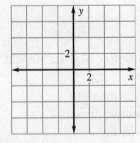

9. $E(-3, 4), F(-1, 4), G(2, 4), H(-1, 1)$;

    $\overline{EG}$ and $\overline{FH}$

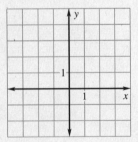

10. $R(3, 5), S(10, 5), T(-4, -3), U(-11, -3)$;

    $\overline{RS}$ and $\overline{TU}$

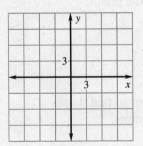

LESSON 1.2 **Practice** *continued*
For use with the lesson "Use Segments and Congruence"

Use the number line to find the indicated distance.

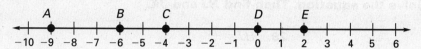

11. *AB*   **12.** *AD*   **13.** *CD*   **14.** *BD*

15. *CE*   **16.** *AE*   **17.** *BE*   **18.** *DE*

In the diagram, points *A*, *B*, *C*, and *D* are collinear, points *C*, *X*, *Y*, and *Z* are collinear, *AB* = *BC* = *CX* = *YZ*, *AD* = 54, *XY* = 22, and *XZ* = 33. Find the indicated length.

19. *AB*

20. *BD*

21. *CY*

22. *CD*

23. *XC*

24. *CZ*

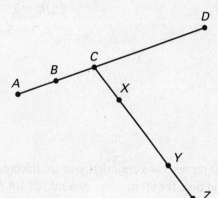

Find the indicated length.

25. Find *ST*.   **26.** Find *AC*.   **27.** Find *NP*.

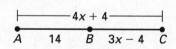
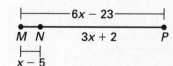

LESSON
1.2 **Practice** *continued*
For use with the lesson "Use Segments and Congruence"

**Point *J* is between *H* and *K* on $\overline{HK}$. Use the given information to write an
equation in terms of *x*. Solve the equation. Then find *HJ* and *JK*.**

28. $HJ = 2x$
$JK = 3x$
$KH = 25$

29. $HJ = \frac{x}{4}$
$JK = 3x - 4$
$KH = 22$

30. $HJ = 5x - 4$
$JK = 8x - 10$
$KH = 38$

31. $HJ = 5x - 3$
$JK = x - 9$
$KH = 5x$

32. Hiking On the map, $\overline{AB}$ represents a trail that you are hiking. You start from the
beginning of the trail and hike for 90 minutes at a rate of 1.4 miles per hour. How
much farther do you need to hike to reach the end of the trail?

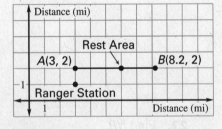

Practice
For use with the lesson "Use Midpoint and Distance Formulas"

1. Line RS bisects $\overline{PQ}$ at point R. Find RQ if $PQ = 14$ centimeters.

2. Line JK bisects $\overline{MN}$ at point J. Find MN if $JM = 6\frac{3}{4}$ feet.

3. Point T bisects $\overline{UV}$. Find UV if $UT = 4\frac{1}{2}$ yards.

4. Point C bisects $\overline{AB}$. Find CB if $AB = 14.8$ meters.

In the diagram, *M* is the midpoint of the segment. Find the indicated length.

5. Find LN.

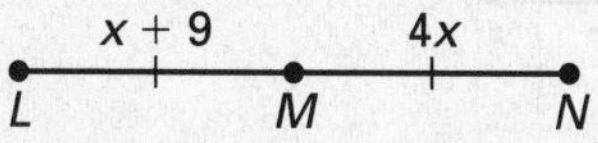

6. Find AM.

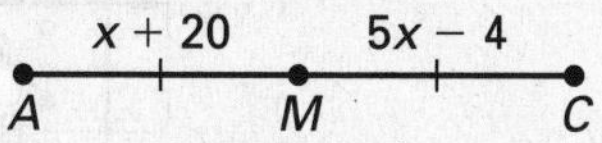

7. Find MR.

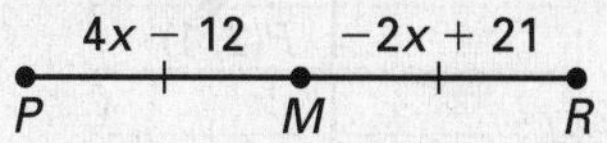

Find the coordinates of the midpoint of the segment with the given endpoints.

8. $S(4, -1)$ and $T(6, 0)$

9. $L(4, 2)$ and $P(0, 2)$

10. $H(-5, 5)$ and $I(7, 3)$

11. $G(-2, -8)$ and $H(-3, -12)$

Use the given endpoint *R* and midpoint *M* of $\overline{RS}$ to find the coordinates of the other endpoint *S*.

12. $R(6, 0)$, $M(0, 2)$

13. $R(3, 4)$, $M(3, -2)$

14. $R(-3, -2)$, $M(-1, -8)$

15. $R(11, -5)$, $M(-4, -4)$

LESSON 1.3 **Practice** *continued*
For use with the lesson "Use Midpoint and Distance Formulas"

Find the length of the segment. Round to the nearest tenth of a unit.

16.
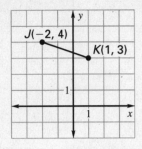

17.
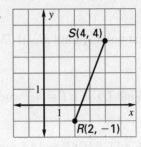

18.
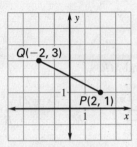

19.
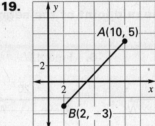

Find the length of the segment. Then find the coordinates of the midpoint of the segment.

20.
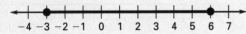

21.
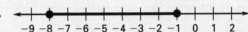

The endpoints of two segments are given. Find each segment length. Tell whether the segments are congruent.

22. $\overline{AB}$: $A(2, 6)$, $B(0, 3)$
    $\overline{CD}$: $C(-1, 0)$, $D(1, 3)$

23. $\overline{RS}$: $R(5, 4)$, $S(0, 4)$
    $\overline{TU}$: $T(-4, -3)$, $U(-1, 1)$

24. $\overline{KL}$: $K(-4, 13)$, $L(-10, 6)$
    $\overline{MN}$: $M(-1, -2)$, $N(-1, -11)$

25. $\overline{OP}$: $O(6, -2)$, $P(3, -2)$
    $\overline{QR}$: $Q(5, 2)$, $R(1, 5)$

Name _____ Date _____

26. **Distances** Your house and the mall are 9.6 miles apart on the same straight road. The movie theater is halfway between your house and the mall, on the same road.

   a. Draw and label a sketch to represent this situation. How far is your house from the movie theater?

   b. You walk at an average speed of 3.2 miles per hour. About how long would it take you to walk to the movie theater from your house?

In Exercises 27–29, use the map. The locations of the towns on the map are: Dunkirk (0, 0), Clearfield (10, 2), Lake City (5, 7), and Allentown (1, 4). The coordinates are given in miles.

27. Find the distance between each pair of towns. Round to the nearest tenth of a mile.

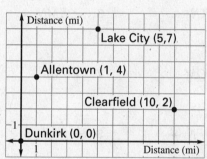

28. Which two towns are closest together? Which two towns are farthest apart?

29. The map is being used to plan a 26-mile marathon. Which of the following plans is the best route for the marathon? *Explain.*

   A. Dunkirk to Clearfield to Allentown to Dunkirk

   B. Dunkirk to Clearfield to Lake City to Allentown to Dunkirk

   C. Dunkirk to Lake City to Clearfield to Dunkirk

   D. Dunkirk to Lake City to Allentown to Dunkirk

Name _____ Date _____

Practice
For use with the lesson "Measure and Classify Angles"

Use a protractor to measure the angle to the nearest degree. Write two names for the angle. Then name the vertex and the sides of the angle.

1.

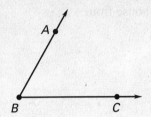

2.

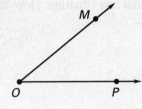

3.

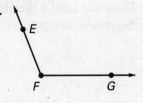

Give another name for the angle in the diagram. Tell whether the angle appears to be *acute, obtuse, right,* or *straight*.

4. $\angle JKN$

5. $\angle KMN$

6. $\angle PQM$

7. $\angle JML$

8. $\angle QPN$

9. $\angle PLK$

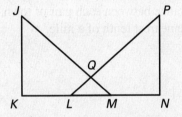

Use the given information to find the indicated angle measure.

10. Given $m\angle ABC = 94°$, find $m\angle CBD$.

11. Given $m\angle QST = 135°$, find $m\angle QSR$.

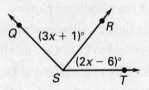

Name _____ Date _____

Find the indicated angle measure.

12. $a°$

13. $b°$

14. $c°$

15. $d°$

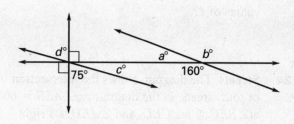

In the diagram, $\overrightarrow{BD}$ bisects $\angle ABC$. Find $m\angle ABC$.

16.

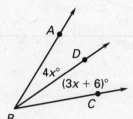

17.

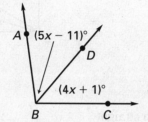

18.

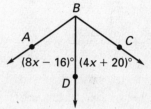

Plot the points in a coordinate plane and draw $\angle ABC$. Classify the angle.
Then give the coordinates of a point that lies in the interior of the angle.

19. $A(2, 3), B(3, 0), C(2, 6)$

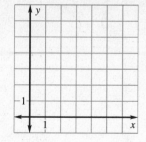

20. $A(6, 2), B(-1, -2), C(2, 3)$

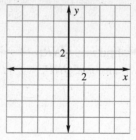

21. $A(-4, -3), B(-1, 3), C(4, 4)$

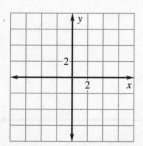

22. $A(-2, -4), B(-2, -1), C(3, -1)$

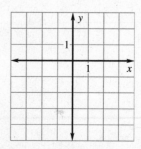

Practice *continued*
For use with the lesson "Measure and Classify Angles"

23. Let $(3x + 24)°$ represent the measure of an obtuse angle. What are the possible values of x?

24. Streets The diagram shows the intersection of four streets. In the diagram, $m\angle AEB = 60°$, $m\angle BEC = m\angle CED$, and $\angle AED$ is a right angle. What is the measure of $\angle CED$?

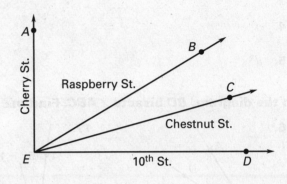

25. Flags In the flag shown, $\angle MNP$ is a straight angle and $\overrightarrow{NR}$ bisects $\angle MNP$ and $\angle QNS$. Use only the labeled angles in the diagram.

a. Which angles are acute? obtuse? right?

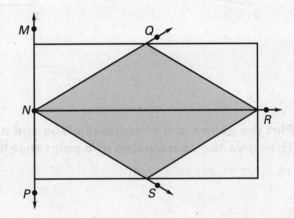

b. Identify the congruent angles.

c. If $m\angle QNR = 30°$, find $m\angle MNR$, $m\angle RNS$, $m\angle QNS$, and $m\angle QNP$.

LESSON 1.5 Practice

For use with the lesson "Describe Angle Pair Relationships"

∠1 and ∠2 are complementary angles and ∠2 and ∠3 are supplementary angles. Given the measure of ∠1, find $m∠2$ and $m∠3$.

1. $m∠1 = 80°$ **2.** $m∠1 = 33°$ **3.** $m∠1 = 72°$ **4.** $m∠1 = 7°$

Find $m∠ABC$ and $m∠CBD$.

5.
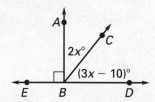

6.
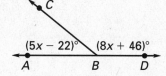

7.
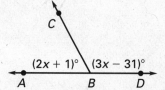

In Exercises 8–12, use the diagram. Tell whether the angles are *vertical angles*, a *linear pair*, or *neither*.

8. ∠1 and ∠3

9. ∠2 and ∠3

10. ∠4 and ∠5

11. ∠5 and ∠8

12. ∠4 and ∠9

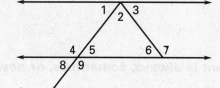

13. The measure of one angle is three times the measure of its complement. Find the measure of each angle.

14. Two angles form a linear pair. The measure of one angle is 8 times the measure of the other angle. Find the measure of each angle.

15. The measure of one angle is 38° less than the measure of its supplement. Find the measure of each angle.

Name _____   Date _____

Practice *continued*
For use with the lesson *"Describe Angle Pair Relationships"*

Find the values of *x* and *y*.

16.
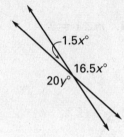
1.5x°
16.5x°
20y°

17.
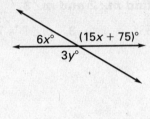
6x°   (15x + 75)°
3y°

18.
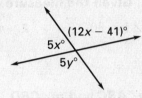
(12x − 41)°
5x°
5y°

19.
(14x + 4)°
(16x − 4)°   (4y − 8)°

20.
(28x − 7)°   (24x + 18)°
(12y + 30)°

21.
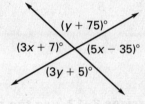
(y + 75)°
(3x + 7)°   (5x − 35)°
(3y + 5)°

Tell whether the statement is *always*, *sometimes*, or *never* true.

22. Two complementary angles form a linear pair.

23. The supplement of an obtuse angle is an acute angle.

24. An angle that has a supplement also has a complement.

∠*A* and ∠*B* are complementary angles. Find *m*∠*A* and *m*∠*B*.

25. $m\angle A = x°$
    $m\angle B = (2x − 75)°$

26. $m\angle A = (4x + 34)°$
    $m\angle B = (x + 36)°$

27. $m\angle A = (4x − 18)°$
    $m\angle B = (6x − 18)°$

28. $m\angle A = (2x + 10)°$
    $m\angle B = (−x + 55)°$

Geometry
Practice Workbook

LESSON 1.5

Practice *continued*

For use with the lesson "Describe Angle Pair Relationships"

∠A and ∠B are supplementary angles. Find *m∠A* and *m∠B*.

29. $m\angle A = (x + 50)°$

$m\angle B = (x + 100)°$

30. $m\angle A = 6x°$

$m\angle B = (x + 5)°$

31. $m\angle A = (2x + 3)°$

$m\angle B = (3x - 223)°$

32. $m\angle A = (-4x + 40)°$

$m\angle B = (x + 50)°$

Roof trusses can have several different layouts. The diagram below shows one type of roof truss made out of beams of wood. Use the diagram to identify two different examples of the indicated type of angle pair. In the diagram, ∠*HBC* and ∠*BCE* are right angles.

33. Supplementary angles

34. Complementary angles

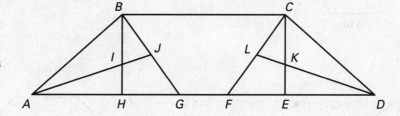

35. Vertical angles

36. Linear pair angles

37. Adjacent angles

38. Angle of elevation An *angle of elevation* is the angle between the horizontal line and the line of sight of an object above the horizontal. In the diagram, a plane is flying horizontally across the sky and ∠*RST* represents the angle of elevation. How is the angle of elevation affected as the plane flies closer to the person? *Explain.*

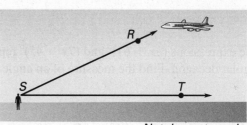

Not drawn to scale

Name _____ Date _____

Practice

For use with the lesson "Classify Polygons"

Tell whether the figure is a polygon. If it is not, explain why. If it is a polygon, tell whether it is *convex* or *concave*.

1.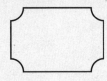

2.

3.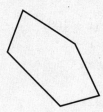

Classify the polygon by the number of sides. Tell whether the polygon is *equilateral, equiangular,* or *regular.* Explain your reasoning.

4.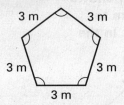
3 m   3 m
3 m   3 m
3 m

5.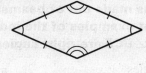

6.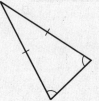

7.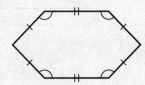

8. The lengths (in feet) of two sides of a regular quadrilateral are represented by the expressions $8x - 6$ and $4x + 22$. Find the length of a side of the quadrilateral.

9. The expressions $(3x + 63)°$ and $(7x - 45)°$ represent the measures of two angles of a regular decagon. Find the measure of an angle of the decagon.

10. The expressions $-2x + 41$ and $7x - 40$ represent the lengths (in kilometers) of two sides of an equilateral pentagon. Find the length of a side of the pentagon.

Name _____ Date _____

Practice *continued*
For use with the lesson *"Classify Polygons"*

Tell whether the statement is *always*, *sometimes*, or *never* true.

11. A quadrilateral is convex.

12. An octagon is regular.

13. A triangle is concave.

14. A regular polygon is equilateral.

Draw a figure that fits the description.

15. A quadrilateral that is not regular

16. A convex heptagon

17. A concave pentagon

18. An equiangular hexagon that is not equilateral

Each figure is a regular polygon. Find the value of *x*.

19.

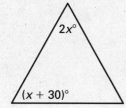

$2x°$

$(x + 30)°$

20.

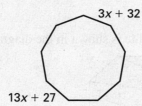

$3x + 32$

$13x + 27$

21.

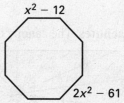

$x^2 - 12$

$2x^2 - 61$

22.

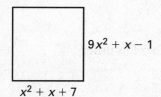

$9x^2 + x - 1$

$x^2 + x + 7$

23.

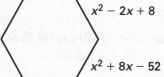

$x^2 - 2x + 8$

$x^2 + 8x - 52$

24.

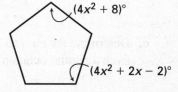

$(4x^2 + 8)°$

$(4x^2 + 2x - 2)°$

Name _____   Date _____

25. The vertices of a figure are given below. Plot and connect the points so that they form a convex polygon. Classify the figure. Then show that the figure is equilateral using algebra.

$A(3, 0)$, $B(3, 6)$, $C(2, 3)$, $D(4, 3)$

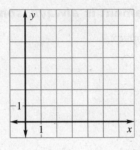

26. **Picture frames** A picture frame with a wooden border is a regular triangle, as shown. You want to decorate the frame by wrapping a ribbon around it. How many feet of ribbon are needed to wrap the ribbon around the border one time?

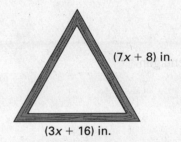

$(7x + 8)$ in.

$(3x + 16)$ in.

27. **Parachutes** The canopy of a parachute is shown in the diagram.

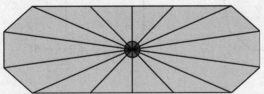

a. Is the shape of the canopy a *convex* or *concave* polygon?

b. Classify the polygon by the number of sides. Then use a ruler and a protractor to determine whether the figure is equilateral, equiangular, or regular.

c. Determine the number of lines of symmetry in the canopy. How does this differ from a regular octagon?

Name _____ Date _____

Sketch the next figure in the pattern.

1.

2.

3.

4.

Describe a pattern in the numbers. Write the next number in the pattern.
Graph the pattern on a number line.

5. 113, 224, 335, 446, . . .

6. 4, 6, 9, 13, 18, . . .

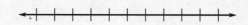

7. $\frac{1}{3}, \frac{3}{4}, \frac{5}{5}, \frac{7}{6}, \cdots$

8. $\frac{7}{8}, \frac{6}{7}, \frac{5}{6}, \frac{4}{5}, \cdots$

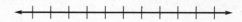

9. 3, 0, −3, −6, . . .

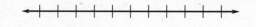

10. 1, 4, 9, 16, . . .

11. 2, 5, 11, 23, . . .

12. 2, 3, 5, 7, 11, . . .

Name _____ Date _____

The first three objects in a pattern are shown. How many squares are in the next object?

13.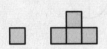

14.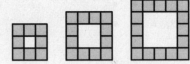

Show the conjecture is false by finding a counterexample.

15. The quotient of two whole numbers is a whole number.

16. The difference of the absolute value of two numbers is positive, meaning $|a| - |b| > 0$.

17. If $m \neq -1$, then $\dfrac{m}{m + 1} < 1$.

18. The square root of a number x is always less than x.

LESSON 2.1

Practice *continued*
For use with the lesson "Use Inductive Reasoning"

Write a function rule relating x and y.

19.

x	1	2	3
y	1	8	27

20.

x	1	2	3
y	−5	−3	−1

21.

x	1	2	3
y	4	3	2

22.

x	1	2	4
y	1	0.5	0.25

23. **Bacteria Growth** Suppose you are studying bacteria in biology class. The table shows the number of bacteria after *n* doubling periods. Your teacher asks you to predict the number of bacteria after 7 doubling periods. What would your prediction be?

n (periods)	0	1	2	3	4	5
billions of bacteria	4	8	16	32	64	128

24. **Chemistry** The half-life of an isotope is the amount of time it takes for half of the isotope to decay. Suppose you begin with 25 grams of Platinum-191, which has a half-life of 3 days. How many days will it take before there is less than 1 gram of the isotope?

LESSON 2.2 Practice

For use with the lesson "Analyze Conditional Statements"

Rewrite the conditional statement in if-then form.

1. It is time for dinner if it is 6 P.M.

2. There are 12 eggs if the carton is full.

3. An obtuse angle is an angle that measures more than 90° and less than 180°.

4. The car runs when there is gas in the tank.

Write the converse, inverse, and contrapositive of each statement.

5. If you like hockey, then you go to the hockey game.

6. If x is odd, then $3x$ is odd.

Decide whether the statement is *true* or *false*. If false, provide a counterexample.

7. The equation $4x - 3 = 12 + 2x$ has exactly one solution.

8. If $x^2 = 36$, then x must equal 18 or -18.

9. If $m\angle A = 122°$, then the measure of the supplement of $\angle A$ is 58°.

10. Two lines intersect in at most one point.

LESSON 2.2

Practice *continued*
For use with the lesson "Analyze Conditional Statements"

Write the converse of each true statement. If the converse is also true, combine the statements to write a true biconditional statement.

11. If an angle measures 30°, then it is acute.

12. If two angles are supplementary, then the sum of their measures is 180°.

13. If two circles have the same diameter, then they have the same circumference.

14. If an animal is a panther, then it lives in the forest.

Rewrite the biconditional statement as a conditional statement and its converse.

15. Two lines are perpendicular if and only if they intersect to form right angles.

16. A point is a midpoint of a segment if and only if it divides the segment into two congruent segments.

Decide whether the statement is a valid definition.

17. If a number is divisible by 2 and 3, then it is divisible by 6.

18. If two angles have the same measure, then they are congruent.

19. If two angles are not adjacent, then they are vertical angles.

LESSON
2.2

Practice *continued*
For use with the lesson "Analyze Conditional Statements"

In Exercises 20–22, use the information in the table to write a definition for each type of saxophone.

Instrument	Frequency (cycles per second)	
	Lower limit (Hz)	Upper limit (Hz)
E-flat baritone saxophone	69	415
B-flat tenor saxophone	103	622
E-flat alto saxophone	138	830

20. E-flat baritone saxophone

21. B-flat tenor saxophone

22. E-flat alto saxophone

In Exercises 23 and 24, use the information in the table above and the answers to Exercise 20–22.

23. If the frequency of a saxophone was 95 Hz, what could you conclude?

24. If the frequency of a saxophone was 210 Hz, what could you conclude?

LESSON 2.3 **Practice**
For use with the lesson "Apply Deductive Reasoning"

Determine if statement (3) follows from statements (1) and (2) by either the Law of Detachment or the Law of Syllogism. If it does, state which law was used. If it does not, write invalid.

1. (1) If an angle measures more than 90°, then it is not acute.

   (2) $m\angle ABC = 120°$

   (3) $\angle ABC$ is not acute.

2. (1) All 45° angles are congruent.

   (2) $\angle A \cong \angle B$

   (3) $\angle A$ and $\angle B$ are 45° angles.

3. (1) If you order the apple pie, then it will be served with ice cream.

   (2) Matthew ordered the apple pie.

   (3) Matthew was served ice cream.

4. (1) If you wear the school colors, then you have school spirit.

   (2) If you have school spirit, then the team feels great.

   (3) If you wear the school colors, then the team will feel great.

5. (1) If you eat too much turkey, then you will get sick.

   (2) Kinsley got sick.

   (3) Kinsley ate too much turkey.

6. (1) If $\angle 2$ is acute, then $\angle 3$ is obtuse.

   (2) If $\angle 3$ is obtuse, then $\angle 4$ is acute.

   (3) If $\angle 2$ is acute, then $\angle 4$ is acute.

LESSON
2.3

Practice *continued*

For use with the lesson "Apply Deductive Reasoning"

In Exercises 7–10, decide whether *inductive* or *deductive* reasoning is used to reach the conclusion. *Explain* your reasoning.

7. Angela knows that Walt is taller than Peter. She also knows that Peter is taller than Natalie. Angela reasons that Walt is taller than Natalie.

8. Josh knows that Brand X computers cost less than Brand Y computers. All other brands that Josh knows of cost less than Brand X. Josh reasons that Brand Y costs more than all other brands.

9. For the past three Wednesdays, the cafeteria has served macaroni and cheese for lunch. Dana concludes that the cafeteria will serve macaroni and cheese for lunch this Wednesday.

10. If you live in Nevada and are between the ages of 16 and 18, then you must take driver's education to get your license. Anthony lives in Nevada, is 16 years old, and has his driver's license. Therefore, Anthony took driver's education.

**In Exercises 11 and 12, state whether the argument is valid.
Explain your reasoning.**

11. Jeff knows that if he does not do his chores in the morning, he will not be allowed to play video games later the same day. Jeff does not play video games on Saturday afternoon. So Jeff did not do his chores on Saturday morning.

12. Katie knows that all sophomores take driver education in her school. Brandon takes driver education. So Brandon is a sophomore.

LESSON 2.3 **Practice** *continued*
For use with the lesson "Apply Deductive Reasoning"

In Exercises 13–16, use the true statements below to determine whether you know the conclusion is *true* or *false*. *Explain* your reasoning.

If Dan goes shopping, then he will buy a pretzel.

If the mall is open, then Jodi and Dan will go shopping.

If Jodi goes shopping, then she will buy a pizza.

The mall is open.

13. Dan bought a pizza.

14. Jodi and Dan went shopping.

15. Jodi bought a pizza.

16. Jodi had some of Dan's pretzel.

17. Robotics Because robots can withstand higher temperatures than humans, a fire-fighting robot is under development. Write the following statements about the robot in order. Then use the Law of Syllogism to complete the statement, "If there is a fire, then __?__."

   A. If the robot sets off the fire alarm, then it concludes there is a fire.

   B. If the robot senses high levels of smoke and heat, then it sets off a fire alarm.

   C. If the robot locates the fire, then the robot extinguishes the fire.

   D. If there is a fire, then the robot senses high levels of smoke and heat.

   E. If the robot concludes there is a fire, then it locates the fire.

Name _____Aobi Blackburn._____ Date _____

Draw a sketch to illustrate each postulate.

1. If two lines intersect, then their intersection is exactly one point.

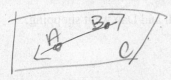

2. If two points lie in a plane, then the line containing them lies in the plane.

3. If two planes intersect, then their intersection is a line.

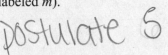

Use the diagram to state and write out the postulate that verifies the truth of the statement.

4. The points *E*, *F*, and *H* lie in a plane (labeled *R*).

postulate 8

5. The points *E* and *F* lie on a line (labeled *m*).

postulate 5

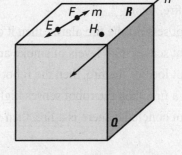

6. The planes *Q* and *R* intersect in a line (labeled *n*).

postulate 11

7. The points *E* and *F* lie in a plane *R*. Therefore, line *m* lies in plane *R*.

postulate 10.

Name _____ Date _____

LESSON 2.4 **Practice** *continued*
For use with the lesson "Use Postulates and Diagrams"

In Exercises 8–11, think of the intersection of the ceiling and the front wall of your classroom as line *k*. Think of the center of the floor as point *A* and the center of the ceiling as point *B*.

8. Is there more than one line that contains both points *A* and *B*?

Postulate 6 (NO)

9. Is there more than one plane that contains both points *A* and *B*?

NO

10. Is there a plane that contains line *k* and point *A*?

yes

11. Is there a plane that contains points *A*, *B*, and a point on the front wall?

yes.

In Exercises 12–19, use the diagram to determine if the statement is *true* or *false*.

12. Points *A*, *B*, *D*, and *J* are coplanar.

False True

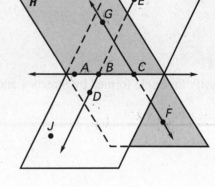

13. ∠*EBA* is a right angle.

True. False

14. Points *E*, *G*, and *A* are collinear.

True. Fals

15. $\overleftrightarrow{FG}$ ⊥ plane *H*

False

16. ∠*ABD* and ∠*EBC* are vertical angles.

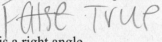
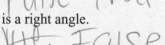
False. True

17. Planes *H* and *K* intersect at $\overleftrightarrow{AB}$.

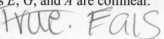
False True.

18. $\overleftrightarrow{FG}$ and $\overleftrightarrow{DE}$ intersect.

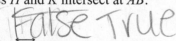
True.

19. ∠*GCA* and ∠*CBD* are congruent angles.

True.

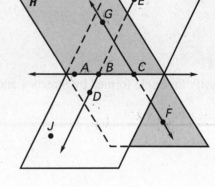

Name _____ Date _____

20. **Neighborhood Map** A friend e-mailed you the following statements about a neighborhood. Use the statements to complete parts (a)–(e).

Building B is due south of Building A.

Buildings A and B are on Street 1.

Building C is due east of Building B.

Buildings B and C are on Street 2.

Building D is southeast of Building B.

Buildings B and D are on Street 3.

Building E is due west of Building C.

$\angle DBE$ formed by Streets 2 and 3 is acute.

a. Draw a diagram of the neighborhood.

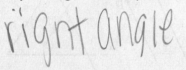

b. Where do Streets 1 and 2 intersect?

Building B

c. Classify the angle formed by Streets 1 and 2.

right angle

d. What street is building E on?

Street 2

e. Is building E between buildings B and C? *Explain*.

yes.

LESSON 2.5

Practice

For use with the lesson "Reason Using Properties from Algebra"

Complete the logical argument by giving a reason for each step.

1. $5(2x - 1) = 9x + 2$ Given

$10x - 5 = 9x + 2$ **a.** _?_ Multiply

$10x = 9x + 7$ **b.** _?_ Subtract 9x from each side.

$x = 7$ **c.** _?_ Divide

2. $8x - 5 = -2x - 15$ Given

$10x - 5 = -15$ **a.** _?_ add -5 to each side.

$10x = -10$ **b.** _?_ Divide -10 by each side

$x = -1$ **c.** _?_

3. $AB = BC$ Given

$AC = AB + BC$ **a.** _?_ Add AB to each side.

$AC = AB + AB$ **b.** _?_ Multiply.

$AC = 2(AB)$ **c.** _?_

4. $m\angle AEB = m\angle CED$ Given

$m\angle BEC = m\angle BEC$ **a.** _?_ Angle measure

$m\angle AEB + m\angle BEC = m\angle CED + m\angle BEC$ **b.** _?_

$m\angle AEC = m\angle AEB + m\angle BEC$ **c.** _?_

$m\angle BED = m\angle CED + m\angle BEC$ **d.** _?_

$m\angle AEC = m\angle BED$ **e.** _?_

5. $\overleftrightarrow{AB} \perp \overleftrightarrow{EF}, \overleftrightarrow{CD} \perp \overleftrightarrow{EF}$ Given

$m\angle 1 = 90°$ **a.** _?_

$m\angle 2 = 90°$ **b.** _?_

$m\angle 1 = m\angle 2$ **c.** _?_

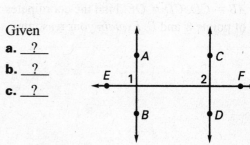

Name _____ Date _____

Practice *continued*
For use with the lesson "Reason Using Properties from Algebra"

Use the property to complete the statement.

6. Reflexive Property of Angle Measure: $m\angle B =$ ___?___.

   $M\angle B$

7. Transitive Property of Equality: If $CD = GH$ and ___?___ $= RS$, then ___?___.

   $GH = RS$ then $CD = GH$.

8. Addition Property of Equality: If $x = 3$, then $14 + x =$ ___?___.

   $14 + 3 = 17$.

9. Symmetric Property of Equality: If $BC = RL$, then ___?___.

   $RL = BC$.

10. Substitution Property of Equality: If $m\angle A = 45°$, then $3(m\angle A) =$ ___?___.

11. Multiplication Property of Equality: If $m\angle A = 45°$, then ___?___ $(m\angle A) = 15°$.

12. **Distance** You are given the following information about the diagram at the right: $AB = CD$, $CD = OE$. Find the coordinates of points C and E. *Explain* your reasoning.

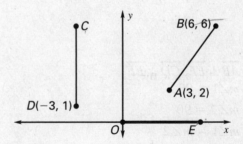

Name _____   Date _____

In Exercises 13–15, use the following information.

Treadmill Mark works out for 45 minutes on a treadmill. He spends t minutes walking and the rest of the time running. He walks 0.06 mi/min and runs 0.11 mi/min. The total distance (in miles) he travels is given by the function $D = 0.06t + 0.11(45 - t)$.

13. Solve the formula for t and write a reason for each step.

14. Make a table that shows the time spent walking for the following distances traveled: 2.7, 3, 3.7, 4.3, and 4.5.

15. Use the table from Exercise 14 to graph the time spent walking as a function of the distance traveled. What happens to the time spent walking as distance increases?

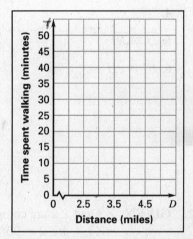

In Exercises 16–18, use the following information.

Statistics The students at a school vote for one of four candidates for class president. The circle graph below shows the results of the election. Each sector on the graph represents the percent of the total votes that each candidate received. You know the following about the circle graph.

$m\angle 1 + m\angle 2 + m\angle 3 + m\angle 4 = 360°$

$m\angle 2 + m\angle 3 = 200°$

$m\angle 1 = m\angle 4$

$m\angle 2 = m\angle 4$

16. Find the angle measure for each sector.

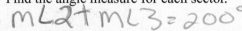

17. What percent of the vote did each candidate receive?

18. How many votes did each candidate receive if there were a total of 315 votes?

LESSON 2.6 Practice
For use with the lesson "Prove Statements about Segments and Angles"

In Exercises 1–4, complete the proof.

1. **GIVEN:** $HI = 9$, $IJ = 9$, $\overline{IJ} \cong \overline{JH}$

   PROVE: $\overline{HI} \cong \overline{JH}$

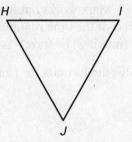

Statements	Reasons
1. $HI = 9$	1. ?
2. $IJ = 9$	2. ?
3. $HI = IJ$	3. ?
4. ?	4. Definition of congruent segments
5. $\overline{IJ} \cong \overline{JH}$	5. ?
6. $\overline{HI} \cong \overline{JH}$	6. ?

2. **GIVEN:** $\angle 3$ and $\angle 2$ are complementary.
   $m\angle 1 + m\angle 2 = 90°$

   PROVE: $\angle 1 \cong \angle 3$

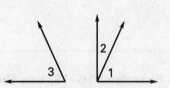

Statements	Reasons
1. $\angle 3$ and $\angle 2$ are complementary.	1. ?
2. $m\angle 1 + m\angle 2 = 90°$	2. ?
3. $m\angle 3 + m\angle 2 = 90°$	3. ?
4. $m\angle 1 + m\angle 2 = m\angle 3 + m\angle 2$	4. ?
5. $m\angle 1 = m\angle 3$	5. ?
6. $\angle 1 \cong \angle 3$	6. ?

**LESSON
2.6**

Practice *continued*

For use with the lesson "Prove Statements about Segments and Angles"

3. **GIVEN:** $AL = SK$

   PROVE: $AS = LK$

   A   L   S   K

Statements	Reasons
1. $AL = SK$	1. _?_
2. $LS = LS$	2. _?_
3. $AL + LS = SK + LS$	3. _?_
4. $AL + LS = AS$	4. _?_
5. $SK + LS = LK$	5. _?_
6. $AS = LK$	6. _?_

4. **GIVEN:** $m\angle 4 = 120°$, $\angle 2 \cong \angle 5$, $\angle 4 \cong \angle 5$

   PROVE: $m\angle 2 = 120°$

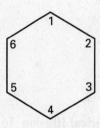

Statements	Reasons
1. $m\angle 4 = 120°$, $\angle 2 \cong \angle 5$, $\angle 4 \cong \angle 5$	1. _?_
2. $\angle 2 \cong \angle 4$	2. _?_
3. _?_	3. Definition of congruent angles
4. $m\angle 2 = 120°$	4. _?_

Name _____ Date _____

Practice *continued*

For use with the lesson "Prove Statements about Segments and Angles"

Solve for *x* using the given information. *Explain* **your steps.**

5. $\angle W \cong \angle Z$

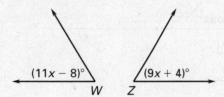

$(11x - 8)°$ $(9x + 4)°$
W   Z

6. $\overline{FG} \cong \overline{FJ}, \overline{FJ} \cong \overline{JH}$

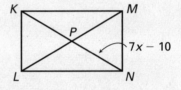

F   J
$5x - 7$ $3x - 1$
G   H

7. $\angle ABD \cong \angle DBE, \angle EBC \cong \angle DBE$

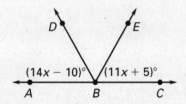

D   E
$(14x - 10)°$ $(11x + 5)°$
A   B   C

8. $\overline{KP} \cong \overline{PN}, KP = 18$

K   M
P
$7x - 10$
L   N

9. Optical Illusion To create the illusion at the right, a special grid was used. In the grid, corresponding row heights are the same measure. For instance, $\overline{UV}$ and $\overline{ZY}$ are congruent. You decide to make this design yourself. You draw the grid, but you need to make sure that the row heights are the same. You measure $\overline{UV}$, $\overline{UW}$, $\overline{ZY}$, and $\overline{ZX}$. You find that $\overline{UV} \cong \overline{ZY}$ and $\overline{UW} \cong \overline{ZX}$. Write an argument that allows you to conclude that $\overline{VW} \cong \overline{YX}$.

Name _____ Date _____

For use with the lesson "Prove Angle Pair Relationships"

Use the diagram to decide whether the statement is *true* or *false*.

1. If $m\angle 1 = 47°$, then $m\angle 2 = 43°$.

2. If $m\angle 1 = 47°$, then $m\angle 3 = 47°$.

3. $m\angle 1 + m\angle 3 = m\angle 2 + m\angle 4$.

4. $m\angle 1 + m\angle 4 = m\angle 2 + m\angle 3$.

Make a sketch of the given information. Label all angles which can be determined.

5. Adjacent complementary angles where one angle measures 42°

6. Nonadjacent supplementary angles where one angle measures 42°

7. Congruent linear pairs

8. Vertical angles which measure 42°

9. $\angle ABC$ and $\angle CBD$ are adjacent complementary angles. $\angle CBD$ and $\angle DBE$ are adjacent complementary angles.

10. $\angle 1$ and $\angle 2$ are complementary. $\angle 3$ and $\angle 4$ are complementary. $\angle 1$ and $\angle 3$ are vertical angles.

LESSON 2.7 **Practice** *continued*
For use with the lesson "Prove Angle Pair Relationships"

Find the value of the variables and the measure of each angle in the diagram.

11.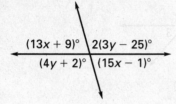

$(13x + 9)°$ $2(3y - 25)°$
$(4y + 2)°$ $(15x - 1)°$

12.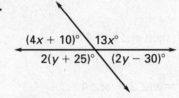

$(4x + 10)°$ $13x°$
$2(y + 25)°$ $(2y - 30)°$

13.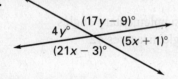

$(17y - 9)°$
$4y°$
$(5x + 1)°$
$(21x - 3)°$

14.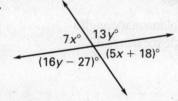

$7x°$ $13y°$
$(16y - 27)°$ $(5x + 18)°$

Give a reason for each step of the proof.

15. GIVEN: $\angle 2 \cong \angle 3$

PROVE: $\angle 1 \cong \angle 4$

Statements	Reasons
1. $\angle 2 \cong \angle 3$	1. _?_
2. $\angle 3 \cong \angle 4$	2. _?_
3. $\angle 2 \cong \angle 4$	3. _?_
4. $\angle 1 \cong \angle 2$	4. _?_
5. $\angle 1 \cong \angle 4$	5. _?_

Name _____ Date _____

Practice *continued*
For use with the lesson "Prove Angle Pair Relationships"

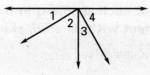

16. GIVEN: $\angle 1$ and $\angle 2$ are complementary.
$\angle 1 \cong \angle 3, \angle 2 \cong \angle 4$

PROVE: $\angle 3$ and $\angle 4$ are complementary.

Statements	Reasons
1. $\angle 1$ and $\angle 2$ are complementary.	1. ?
2. $m\angle 1 + m\angle 2 = 90°$	2. ?
3. $\angle 1 \cong \angle 3, \angle 2 \cong \angle 4$	3. ?
4. $m\angle 1 = m\angle 3, m\angle 2 = m\angle 4$	4. ?
5. $m\angle 3 + m\angle 2 = 90°$	5. ?
6. $m\angle 3 + m\angle 4 = 90°$	6. ?
7. $\angle 3$ and $\angle 4$ are complementary.	7. ?

In the diagram, $\angle 1$ is a right angle and $m\angle 6 = 36°$. Complete the statement with <, >, or =.

17. $m\angle 6 + m\angle 7$ __?__ $m\angle 4 + m\angle 5$

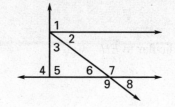

18. $m\angle 6 + m\angle 8$ __?__ $m\angle 2 + m\angle 3$

19. $m\angle 9$ __?__ $3(m\angle 6)$

20. $m\angle 2 + m\angle 3$ __?__ $m\angle 1$

Name _____   Date _____

Think of each segment in the diagram as part of a line. Complete the statement with *parallel*, *skew*, or *perpendicular*.

1. $\overleftrightarrow{WZ}$ and $\overleftrightarrow{ZR}$ are ___?___.

2. $\overleftrightarrow{WZ}$ and $\overleftrightarrow{ST}$ are ___?___.

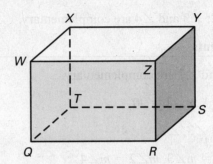

3. $\overleftrightarrow{QT}$ and $\overleftrightarrow{YS}$ are ___?___.

4. Plane *WZR* and plane *SYZ* are ___?___.

5. Plane *RQT* and plane *YXW* are ___?___.

Think of each segment in the diagram as part of a line. Which line(s) or plane(s) appear to fit the description?

6. Line(s) parallel to $\overleftrightarrow{EH}$

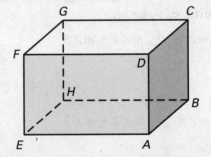

7. Line(s) perpendicular to $\overleftrightarrow{EH}$

8. Line(s) skew to $\overleftrightarrow{CD}$ and containing point *F*

9. Plane(s) perpendicular to plane *AEH*

10. Plane(s) parallel to plane *FGC*

Name _____ Date _____

Practice *continued*
For use with the lesson "Identify Pairs of Lines and Angles"

Classify the angle pair as *corresponding*, *alternate interior*, *alternate exterior*, or *consecutive interior* angles.

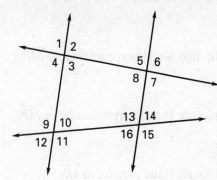

11. $\angle 1$ and $\angle 9$

12. $\angle 8$ and $\angle 13$

13. $\angle 6$ and $\angle 16$

14. $\angle 4$ and $\angle 10$

15. $\angle 8$ and $\angle 16$

16. $\angle 10$ and $\angle 13$

In Exercises 17–20, use the markings in the diagram.

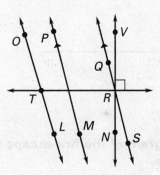

17. Name a pair of parallel lines.

18. Name a pair of perpendicular lines.

19. Is $\overleftrightarrow{OL} \parallel \overleftrightarrow{TR}$? *Explain.*

20. Is $\overleftrightarrow{OL} \perp \overleftrightarrow{TR}$? *Explain.*

Copy and complete the statement with *sometimes*, *always*, or *never*.

21. If two lines are parallel, then they __?__ intersect.

22. If one line is skew to another, then they are __?__ coplanar.

23. If two lines intersect, then they are __?__ perpendicular.

24. If two lines are coplanar, then they are __?__ parallel.

Name _____ Date _____

Copy the diagram and sketch the line.

25. Line through M and parallel to $\overleftrightarrow{NP}$.

26. Line through N and perpendicular to $\overleftrightarrow{MP}$.

27. Line through M and perpendicular to $\overleftrightarrow{MP}$.

28. Line through P and parallel to $\overleftrightarrow{MN}$.

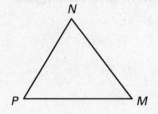

Use construction tools to construct a line through point P that is parallel to line m.

29. • P

m

30. • P

m

Use the diagram of the fire escape to decide whether the statement is *true* or *false*.

31. The planes containing the platforms outside of each pair of windows are parallel to the ground.

32. The planes containing the stairs are parallel to each other.

33. The planes containing the platforms outside of each pair of windows are perpendicular to the planes containing the stairs.

34. The planes containing the platforms outside of each pair of windows are perpendicular to the plane containing the side of the building with the fire escape.

Practice

For use with the lesson "Use Parallel Lines and Transversals"

LESSON 3.2

Find the angle measure. Tell which postulate or theorem you use.

1. If $m\angle 1 = 50°$, then $m\angle 5 =$ _?_.

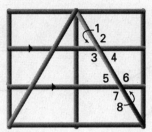

2. If $m\angle 4 = 45°$, then $m\angle 6 =$ _?_.

3. If $m\angle 2 = 130°$, then $m\angle 7 =$ _?_.

4. If $m\angle 6 = 123°$, then $m\angle 3 =$ _?_.

Find $m\angle 1$ and $m\angle 2$.

5.

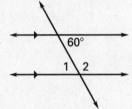

6.

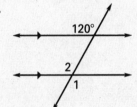

7.

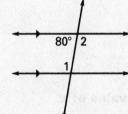

8.

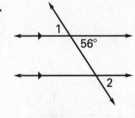

9.

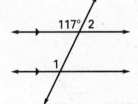

10.

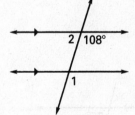

LESSON 3.2

Practice *continued*

For use with the lesson "Use Parallel Lines and Transversals"

Find the values of *x* and *y*.

11.

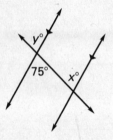

12.

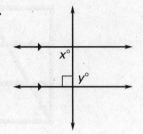

13.

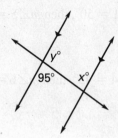

14.

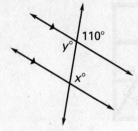

15.

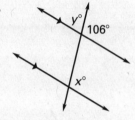

16.

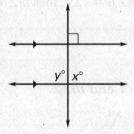

Find the value of *x*.

17.

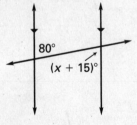

18.

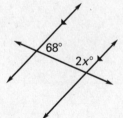

19.

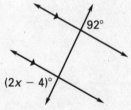

20.

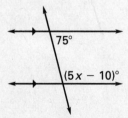

21.

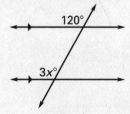

22.

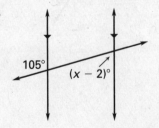

Name _____ Date _____

In Exercises 23–31, complete the two-column proof.

GIVEN: $p \perp q$, $q \parallel r$

PROVE: $p \perp r$

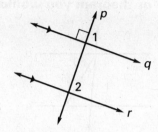

Statements	Reasons	
$p \perp q$	**23.**	?
$\angle 1$ is a right angle.	**24.**	?
$m\angle 1 = 90°$	**25.**	?
$q \parallel r$	**26.**	?
$\angle 1 \cong \angle 2$	**27.**	?
$m\angle 1 = m\angle 2$	**28.**	?
$m\angle 2 = 90°$	**29.**	?
$\angle 2$ is a right angle.	**30.**	?
$p \perp r$	**31.**	?

LESSON 3.3 Practice

For use with the lesson "Prove Lines are Parallel"

Is there enough information to prove that lines *p* and *q* are parallel? If so, state the postulate or theorem you would use.

1.

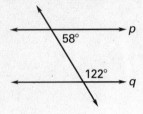

2.

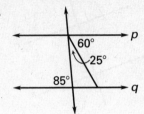

3.

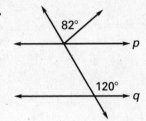

Find the value of *x* that makes *m* ∥ *n*.

4.

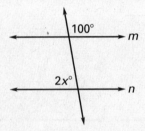

5.

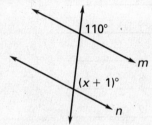

6.

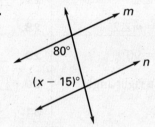

7.

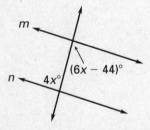

8.

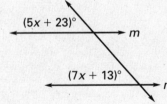

9.

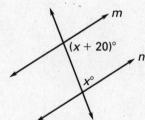

LESSON 3.3 **Practice** *continued*
For use with the lesson "Prove Lines are Parallel"

In Exercises 10–12, choose the word that best completes the statement.

10. If two lines are cut by a transversal so the alternate interior angles are (*congruent, supplementary, complementary*), then the lines are parallel.

11. If two lines are cut by a transversal so the consecutive interior angles are (*congruent, supplementary, complementary*), then the lines are parallel.

12. If two lines are cut by a transversal so the corresponding angles are (*congruent, supplementary, complementary*), then the lines are parallel.

13. **Gardens** A garden has five rows of vegetables. Each row is parallel to the row immediately next to it. *Explain* why the first row is parallel to the last row.

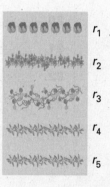

In Exercises 14–18, complete the two-column proof.

GIVEN: $g \parallel h$, $\angle 1 \cong \angle 2$

PROVE: $p \parallel r$

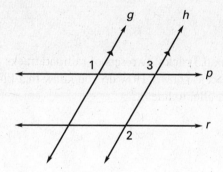

Statements	Reasons
$g \parallel h$	14. _____?_____
$\angle 1 \cong \angle 3$	15. _____?_____
$\angle 1 \cong \angle 2$	16. _____?_____
$\angle 2 \cong \angle 3$	17. _____?_____
$p \parallel r$	18. _____?_____

LESSON 3.3

Practice continued
For use with the lesson "Prove Lines are Parallel"

In Exercises 19–23, complete the two-column proof.

GIVEN: $n \parallel m$, $\angle 1 \cong \angle 2$

PROVE: $p \parallel r$

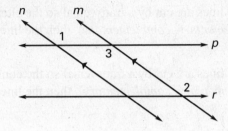

Statements	Reasons
$n \parallel m$	**19.** _____?_____
$\angle 1 \cong \angle 3$	**20.** _____?_____
$\angle 1 \cong \angle 2$	**21.** _____?_____
$\angle 2 \cong \angle 3$	**22.** _____?_____
$p \parallel r$	**23.** _____?_____

24. Railroad Tracks Two sets of railroad tracks
intersect as shown. How do you know that line
n is parallel to line m?

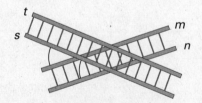

Name _____   Date _____

Practice

For use with the lesson "Find and Use Slopes of Lines"

Find the slope of the line that passes through the points.

1.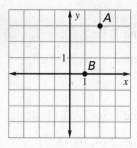

2.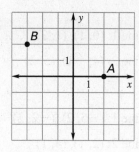

3.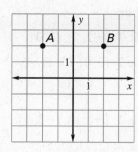

Find the slope of each line. Are the lines parallel?

4.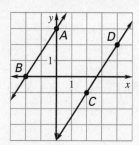

5.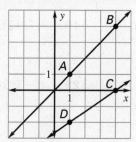

6.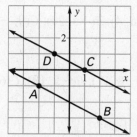

Find the slope of each line. Are the lines perpendicular?

7.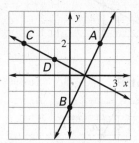

8.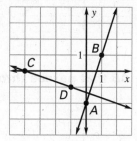

9.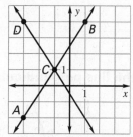

LESSON 3.4 Practice *continued*
For use with the lesson "Find and Use Slopes of Lines"

Tell whether the lines through the given points are *parallel*, *perpendicular*, or *neither*.

10. Line 1: $(-1, 2), (2, 3)$
   Line 2: $(0, 0), (3, 1)$

11. Line 1: $(0, 1), (1, 3)$
   Line 2: $(4, -1), (5, 2)$

12. Line 1: $(-5, 0), (-3, -2)$
   Line 2: $(-2, 2), (0, 4)$

13. Line 1: $(-3, 4), (-3, 1)$
   Line 2: $(2, 1), (5, 5)$

14. Line 1: $(-5, 2), (-2, 2)$
   Line 2: $(2, 1), (4, 1)$

15. Line 1: $(-2, 5), (1, 4)$
   Line 2: $(4, 0), (5, 3)$

Tell whether the intersection of $\overleftrightarrow{AB}$ and $\overleftrightarrow{CD}$ forms a right angle.

16. $A(-8, 3), B(1, 2), C(0, 9), D(-1, 0)$

17. $A(3, 2), B(5, 10), C(7, -4), D(3, -3)$

18. $A(5, 4), B(-3, 20), C(9, -2), D(6, 4)$

19. $A(7, 12), B(1, 5), C(10, -7), D(3, -1)$

20. $A(-8, 17), B(-5, 18), C(6, 11), D(5, 8)$

21. $A(-7, 3), B(-10, 15), C(-1, 5), D(4, 35)$

Graph the line parallel to line *AB* that passes through point *P*.

22.
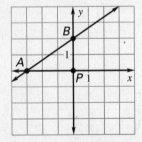

23.
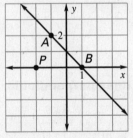

24.
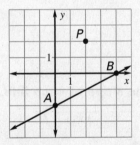

Graph the line perpendicular to line *AB* that passes through point *P*.

25.
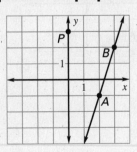

26.
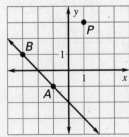

27.
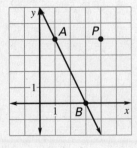

LESSON 3.4

Practice continued
For use with the lesson "Find and Use Slopes of Lines"

In Exercises 28 and 29, consider the three given lines.

Line a: through the points $(2, 0)$ and $(0, 1)$

Line b: through the points $(2, 0)$ and $(0, 5)$

Line c: through the points $(2, 0)$ and $(0, 3)$

28. Which line is most steep?

29. Which line is least steep?

30. Parallelograms A parallelogram is a four-sided figure whose opposite sides are parallel. *Explain* why the figure shown is a parallelogram.

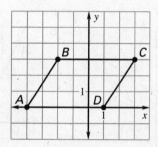

31. Escalators On an escalator, you move 2 feet vertically for every 3 feet you move horizontally. When you reach the top of the escalator, you have moved a horizontal distance of 90 feet. Find the height h of the escalator.

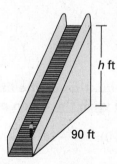

LESSON 3.5 **Practice**
For use with the lesson "Write and Graph Equations of Lines"

Write an equation of line *AB* in slope-intercept form.

1.
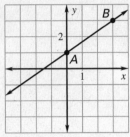

2.
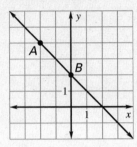

3.
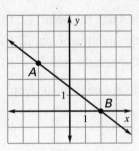

4.
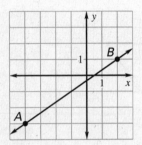

5.
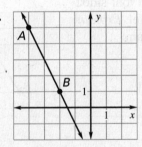

6.
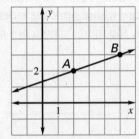

Write an equation of the line that passes through point *P* and is parallel to the line with the given equation.

7. $P(-2, 0); y = -\dfrac{1}{2}x + 6$ **8.** $P(3, 9); y = 4x - 8$ **9.** $P(-5, -4); y = -2x - 10$

Name _____ Date _____

Write an equation of the line that passes through point *P* and is perpendicular to the line with the given equation.

10. $P(5, 20);\ y = \frac{1}{2}x + 8$ **11.** $P(4, 5);\ y = -\frac{1}{3}x - 6$ **12.** $P(3, 5);\ y = 4$

Write an equation of the line that passes through point *P* and is parallel to line *AB*.

13.
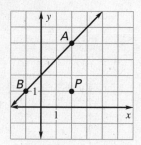

14.
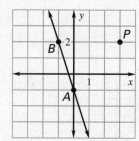

15.
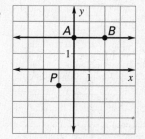

Write an equation of the line that passes through point *P* and is perpendicular to line *AB*.

16.
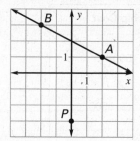

17.
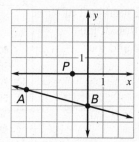

18.
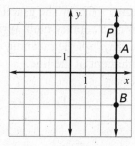

LESSON 3.5

Practice *continued*

For use with the lesson "Write and Graph Equations of Lines"

Graph the equation.

19. $-2x + y = -1$

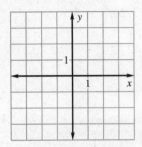

20. $y - 3 = -3x + 2$

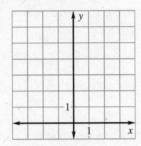

21. $y + 6 = 4$

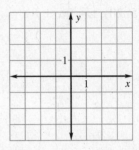

22. $2(x - 1) = -y$

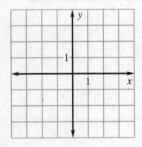

23. $x - 4 = 0$

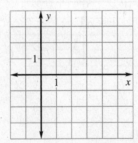

24. $2y - 4 = 2x$

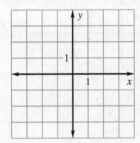

25. Country Club The graph models the total cost of joining a country club. Write an equation of the line. *Explain* the meaning of the slope and the *y*-intercept of the line.

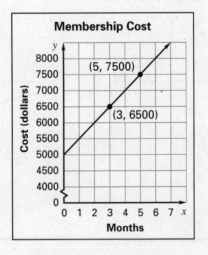

Geometry

LESSON 3.6 **Practice**
For use with the lesson "Prove Theorems about Perpendicular Lines"

What can you conclude from the given information? State the reason for your conclusion.

1. $\angle 1 \cong \angle 2$

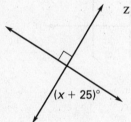

2. $n \perp m$

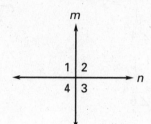

3. $\vec{BA} \perp \vec{BC}$

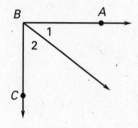

Find the value of x.

4.

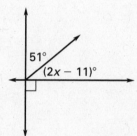

5.

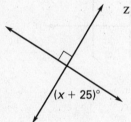

6.

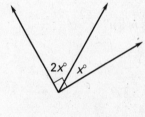

7.

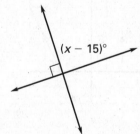

8.

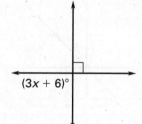

9.

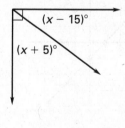

<table>
<tr><td>LESSON
3.6</td><td>**Practice** *continued*
For use with the lesson "Prove Theorems about Perpendicular Lines"</td></tr>
</table>

Find the measure of the indicated angle.

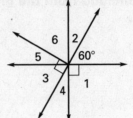

10. $\angle 1$

11. $\angle 2$

12. $\angle 3$

13. $\angle 4$

14. $\angle 5$

15. $\angle 6$

In Exercises 16–18, use the diagram.

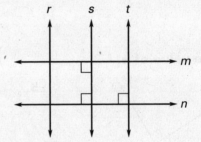

16. Is $r \parallel s$?

17. Is $m \parallel n$?

18. Is $s \parallel t$?

Find the distance from point *A* to line *c*. Round your answers to the nearest tenth.

19.

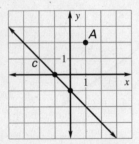

20.

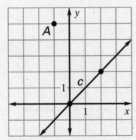

21.

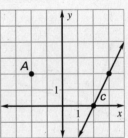

LESSON 3.6

Practice *continued*
For use with the lesson "Prove Theorems about Perpendicular Lines"

22.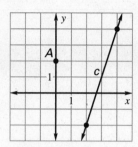

23.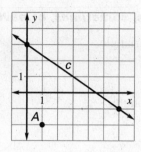

24.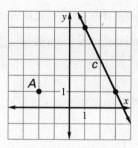

25. **Maps** A map of a neighborhood is drawn on a graph where units are measured in feet.

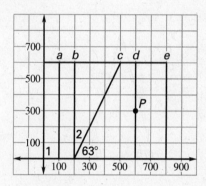

a. Find $m\angle 1$.

b. Find $m\angle 2$.

c. Find the distance from point P to line a.

d. Find the distance from point P to line c. Round your answer to the nearest foot.

Name _____   Date _____

Complete the sentence with *always*, *sometimes*, or *never*.

1. An isosceles triangle is __?__ a right triangle.

2. An obtuse triangle is __?__ a right triangle.

3. A right triangle is __?__ an equilateral triangle.

4. A right triangle is __?__ an isosceles triangle.

Classify the triangle by its sides and by its angles.

5.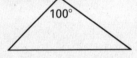

6.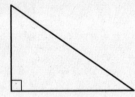

7.

A triangle has the given vertices. Graph the triangle and classify it by its sides. Then determine if it is a right triangle.

8. $A(3, 1)$, $B(3, 4)$, $C(7, 1)$

9. $A(1, 1)$, $B(4, 0)$, $C(8, 5)$

10. $A(2, 2)$, $B(6, 2)$, $C(4, 8)$

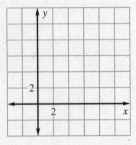

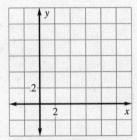

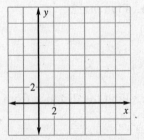

Name _____ Date _____

Find the value of x. Then classify the triangle by its angles.

11.

12.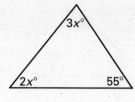

13.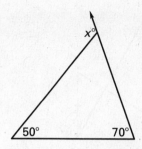

Find the measure of the exterior angle shown.

14.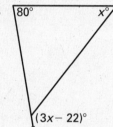

15.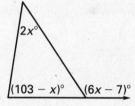

16.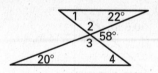

Find the measure of the numbered angle.

17. ∠1

18. ∠2

19. ∠3

20. ∠4

21. In △ABC, m∠A = m∠B + 30° and m∠C = m∠B + 60°. Find the measure of each angle.

22. In △ABC, m∠A = 2(m∠B) and m∠C = 3(m∠B). Find the measure of each angle.

Name _____   Date _____

Find the values of x and y.

23.

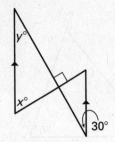

24.

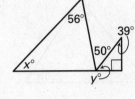

25.

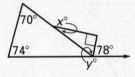

26. Metal Brace The diagram shows the dimensions of a metal brace used for strengthening a vertical and horizontal wooden junction. Classify the triangle formed by its sides. Then copy the triangle, measure the angles, and classify the triangle by its angles.

10.5 in.

7.14 in.

7.7 in.

Date _____

Practice
For use with the lesson "Apply Congruence and Triangles"

1. Copy the congruent triangles shown at the right. Then label the vertices of your triangles so that △*AMT* ≅ △*CDN*. Identify all pairs of congruent corresponding angles and corresponding sides.

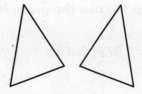

In the diagram, △ *TJM* ≅ △ *PHS*. Complete the statement.

2. ∠*P* ≅ __?__

3. $\overline{JM}$ ≅ __?__

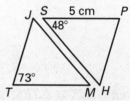

4. m∠*M* = __?__

5. m∠*P* = __?__

6. *MT* = __?__

7. △*HPS* ≅ __?__

Write a congruence statement for any figures that can be proved congruent. *Explain* your reasoning.

8.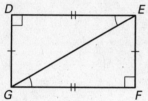

9.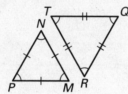

10.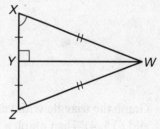

Find the value of x.

11.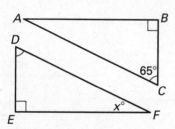

12.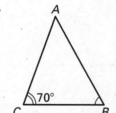

Name _____   Date _____

**In Exercises 13 and 14, use the given information to find the
indicated values.**

13. Given $\triangle ABC \cong \triangle DEF$, find the
values of x and y.

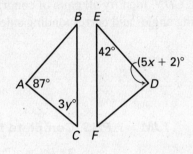

14. Given $\triangle HJK \cong \triangle TRS$, find the
values of a and b.

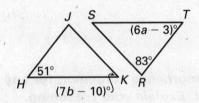

15. Graph the triangle with vertices $A(1, 2)$, $B(7, 2)$,
and $C(5, 4)$. Then graph a triangle congruent
to $\triangle ABC$.

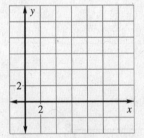

LESSON 4.2 **Practice** *continued*
For use with the lesson "Apply Congruence and Triangles"

16. **Proof** Complete the proof.

GIVEN: $\angle ABD \cong \angle CDB$, $\angle ADB \cong \angle CBD$,
$\overline{AD} \cong \overline{BC}$, $\overline{AB} \cong \overline{DC}$

PROVE: $\triangle ABD \cong \triangle CDB$

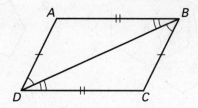

Statements	Reasons
1. $\angle ABD \cong \angle CDB$, $\angle ADB \cong \angle CBD$, $\overline{AD} \cong \overline{BC}$, $\overline{AB} \cong \overline{DC}$	1. Given
2. $\overline{BD} \cong \overline{BD}$	2. __?__
3. __?__	3. Third Angles Theorem
4. $\triangle ABD \cong \triangle CDB$	4. __?__

17. **Carpet Designs** A carpet is made of congruent triangles. One triangular shape is used to make all of the triangles in the design. Which property guarantees that all the triangles are congruent?

Name _____   Date _____

Practice
For use with the lesson "Transformations and Congruence"

Identify the transformation you can use to move figure A onto figure B.

1.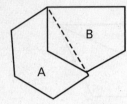

2.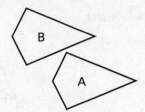

3.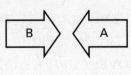

Copy the figure. Draw an example of the effect of the given transformation on the figure.

4. translation

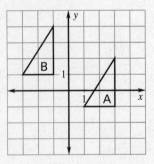

5. reflection

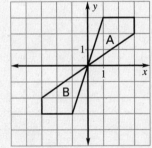

6. rotation

Tell whether a rigid motion can move figure A onto figure B. If so, describe the transformation(s) that you can use. If not, explain why the figures are not congruent.

7.

8.

9.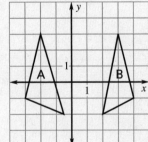

LESSON 4.3

Practice *continued*
For use with the lesson "Transformations and Congruence"

10.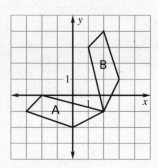

11.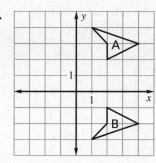

12.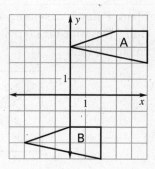

Designs for windows are shown below. Describe the rigid motion(s) that can be used to move figure A onto figure B.

13.

14.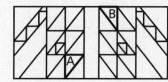

15. Clothing Design Mario created a metal chain belt with congruent links as shown. Describe a combination of transformations that can be used to move link A to link B.

LESSON 4.3

Practice *continued*

For use with the lesson "Transformations and Congruence"

16. Flags Kiley is designing a flag for the school's drill team, the Bolts. Describe the combination of transformations she used to create the flag.

17. Toys A toy manufacturer wants to design a forklift truck similar to the one shown. Describe a combination of transformations that can be used to move part A to part B.

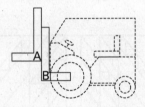

Identify the type of rigid motion represented by the function notation. If the function notation does not represent a rigid motion, write *none*.

18. $(x, y) \rightarrow (x, -y)$

19. $(x, y) \rightarrow (2x, 2y)$

20. $(x, y) \rightarrow (-y, x)$

21. $(x, y) \rightarrow (x + 4, y - 1)$

Name _____ Date _____

Decide whether the congruence statement is true. *Explain* your reasoning.

1. $\triangle ABD \cong \triangle CDB$

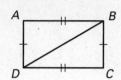

2. $\triangle RST \cong \triangle RQT$

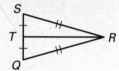

3. $\triangle ABC \cong \triangle DEF$

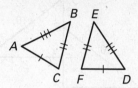

Use the given coordinates to determine if $\triangle ABC \cong \triangle DEF$.

4. $A(1, 2)$, $B(4, -3)$, $C(2, 5)$, $D(4, 7)$, $E(7, 2)$, $F(5, 10)$

5. $A(1, 1)$, $B(4, 0)$, $C(7, 5)$, $D(4, -5)$, $E(6, -6)$, $F(9, -1)$

6. $A(2, -2)$, $B(5, 1)$, $C(4, 8)$, $D(7, 5)$, $E(10, 8)$, $F(9, 13)$

7. $A(-3, 0)$, $B(6, 2)$, $C(-1, 9)$, $D(4, -10)$, $E(13, -8)$, $F(6, -1)$

Decide whether the figure is stable. *Explain* your reasoning.

8.

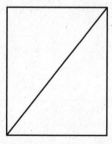

9.

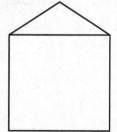

10.

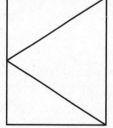

Name _____ Date _____

Practice *continued*

For use with the lesson "Prove Triangles Congruent by SSS"

Determine whether △ *ABC* ≅ △ *DEF*. **Explain** your reasoning.

11.

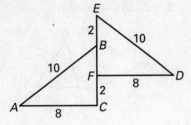

12.

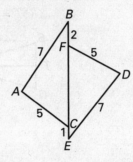

13. **Proof** Complete the proof.

GIVEN: $\overline{AB} \cong \overline{CD}$, $\overline{BC} \cong \overline{AD}$

PROVE: △ *ABC* ≅ △ *CDA*

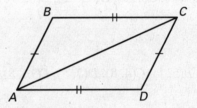

Statements	Reasons
1. $\overline{AB} \cong \overline{CD}$	**1.** _?_
2. $\overline{BC} \cong \overline{AD}$	**2.** _?_
3. $\overline{AC} \cong \overline{AC}$	**3.** _?_
4. △ *ABC* ≅ △ *CDA*	**4.** _?_

Name _____   Date _____

Practice *continued*
For use with the lesson "Prove Triangles Congruent by SSS"

14. **Proof** Complete the proof.

   GIVEN: $\overline{AB} \cong \overline{CB}$, D is the midpoint of $\overline{AC}$.

   PROVE: $\triangle ABD \cong \triangle CBD$

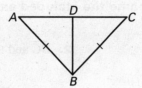

Statements	Reasons
1. $\overline{AB} \cong \overline{CB}$	1. ?
2. D is the midpoint of $\overline{AC}$.	2. ?
3. $\overline{AD} \cong \overline{CD}$	3. ?
4. $\overline{BD} \cong \overline{BD}$	4. ?
5. $\triangle ABD \cong \triangle CBD$	5. ?

15. **Picture Frame** The backs of two different picture frames are shown below. Which picture frame is stable? *Explain* your reasoning.

   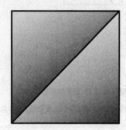

Name _____   Date _____

Practice

For use with the lesson "Prove Triangles Congruent by SAS and HL"

Use the diagram to name the included angle between the given pair of sides.

1. $\overline{AB}$ and $\overline{BC}$

2. $\overline{BC}$ and $\overline{CD}$

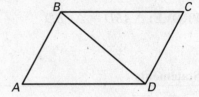

3. $\overline{AB}$ and $\overline{BD}$

4. $\overline{BD}$ and $\overline{DA}$

5. $\overline{DA}$ and $\overline{AB}$

6. $\overline{CD}$ and $\overline{DB}$

Decide whether enough information is given to prove that the triangles are congruent using the SAS Congruence Postulate.

7. $\triangle MAE, \triangle TAE$

8. $\triangle DKA, \triangle SKT$

9. $\triangle JRM, \triangle JTM$

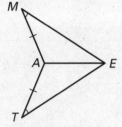
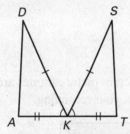
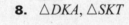
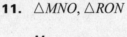
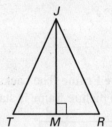

Decide whether enough information is given to prove that the triangles are congruent. If there is enough information, state the congruence postulate or theorem you would use.

10. $\triangle ABC, \triangle DEF$

11. $\triangle MNO, \triangle RON$

12. $\triangle ABC, \triangle ADC$

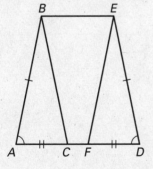
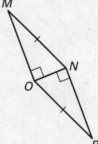
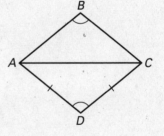

LESSON 4.5 **Practice** *continued*
For use with the lesson "Prove Triangles Congruent by SAS and HL"

State the third congruence that must be given to prove that △JRM ≅ △DFB using the indicated postulate.

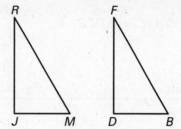

13. **GIVEN:** $\overline{JR} \cong \overline{DF}, \overline{JM} \cong \overline{DB},$ __?__ ≅ __?__
     Use the SSS Congruence Postulate.

14. **GIVEN:** $\overline{JR} \cong \overline{DF}, \overline{JM} \cong \overline{DB},$ __?__ ≅ __?__
     Use the SAS Congruence Postulate.

15. **GIVEN:** $\overline{RM} \cong \overline{FB},$ ∠J is a right angle and
     ∠J ≅ ∠D, __?__ ≅ __?__
     Use the HL Congruence Theorem.

16. **Proof** Complete the proof.

    GIVEN: B is the midpoint of $\overline{AE}$.
    B is the midpoint of $\overline{CD}$.

    PROVE: △ABD ≅ △EBC

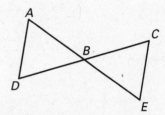

Statements	Reasons
1. B is the midpoint of $\overline{AE}$.	1. __?__
2. __?__	2. Definition of midpoint
3. B is the midpoint of $\overline{CD}$.	3. __?__
4. __?__	4. Definition of midpoint
5. ∠ABD ≅ ∠EBC	5. __?__
6. △ABD ≅ △EBC	6. __?__

LESSON
4.5

Practice *continued*

For use with the lesson "Prove Triangles Congruent by SAS and HL"

17. Proof Complete the proof.

GIVEN: $\overline{AB} \parallel \overline{CD}$, $\overline{AB} \cong \overline{CD}$

PROVE: $\triangle ABC \cong \triangle DCB$

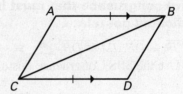

Statements	Reasons
1. $\overline{AB} \parallel \overline{CD}$	**1.** ?
2. $\angle ABC \cong \angle DCB$	**2.** ?
3. $\overline{AB} \cong \overline{CD}$	**3.** ?
4. $\overline{CB} \cong \overline{CB}$	**4.** ?
5. $\triangle ABC \cong \triangle DCB$	**5.** ?

LESSON 4.6

Practice
For use with the lesson "Prove Triangles Congruent by ASA and AAS"

State the third congruence that is needed to prove that △DEF ≅ △MNO using the given postulate or theorem.

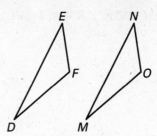

1. **GIVEN:** $\overline{DE} \cong \overline{MN}$, $\angle M \cong \angle D$, __?__ ≅ __?__
   Use the SAS Congruence Postulate.

2. **GIVEN:** $\overline{FE} \cong \overline{ON}$, $\angle F \cong \angle O$, __?__ ≅ __?__
   Use the AAS Congruence Theorem.

3. **GIVEN:** $\overline{DF} \cong \overline{MO}$, $\angle F \cong \angle O$, __?__ ≅ __?__
   Use the ASA Congruence Postulate.

State the third congruence that is needed to prove that △ABC ≅ △XYZ using the given postulate or theorem.

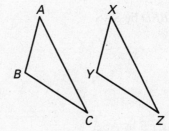

4. **GIVEN:** $\angle A \cong \angle X$, $\angle B \cong \angle Y$, __?__ ≅ __?__
   Use the AAS Congruence Theorem.

5. **GIVEN:** $\angle A \cong \angle X$, $\overline{AB} \cong \overline{XY}$, __?__ ≅ __?__
   Use the ASA Congruence Postulate.

6. **GIVEN:** $\overline{BC} \cong \overline{YZ}$, $\angle C \cong \angle Z$, __?__ ≅ __?__
   Use the AAS Congruence Theorem.

Is it possible to prove that the triangles are congruent? If so, state the postulate(s) or theorem(s) you would use.

7.
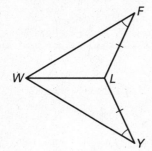

8.
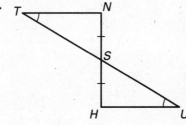

9.
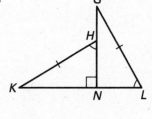

LESSON
4.6

Practice *continued*
For use with the lesson "Prove Triangles Congruent by ASA and AAS"

Tell whether you can use the given information to determine whether
$\triangle JRM \cong \triangle XYZ$. **Explain** your reasoning.

10. $\overline{JM} \cong \overline{XZ}, \angle M \cong \angle Z, \angle R \cong \angle Y$

11. $\overline{JM} \cong \overline{XZ}, \overline{JR} \cong \overline{XY}, \angle J \cong \angle X$

12. $\angle J \cong \angle X, \angle M \cong \angle Z, \angle R \cong \angle Y$

13. $\angle M \cong \angle Z, \angle R \cong \angle Y, \overline{JM} \cong \overline{XY}$

Explain how you can prove that the indicated triangles are congruent
using the given postulate or theorem.

14. $\triangle BEF \cong \triangle BED$ by SAS

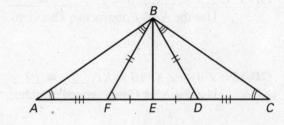

15. $\triangle ADB \cong \triangle CFB$ by ASA

16. $\triangle AFB \cong \triangle CDB$ by AAS

LESSON 4.6 **Practice** *continued*
For use with the lesson "Prove Triangles Congruent by ASA and AAS"

17. Proof Complete the proof.

GIVEN: $\overline{WU} \parallel \overline{YV}, \overline{XU} \parallel \overline{ZV}, \overline{WX} \cong \overline{YZ}$

PROVE: $\triangle WXU \cong \triangle YZV$

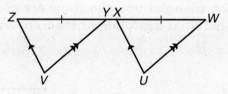

Statements	Reasons
1. $\overline{WU} \parallel \overline{YV}$	1. ___?___
2. $\angle UWX \cong \angle VYZ$	2. ___?___
3. $\overline{XU} \parallel \overline{ZV}$	3. ___?___
4. $\angle UXW \cong \angle VZY$	4. ___?___
5. $\overline{WX} \cong \overline{YZ}$	5. ___?___
6. $\triangle WXU \cong \triangle YZV$	6. ___?___

18. Proof Write a proof.

GIVEN: $\angle B \cong \angle D, \overline{AC} \cong \overline{DC}$

PROVE: $\triangle ABC \cong \triangle EDC$

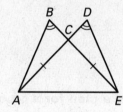

Name _____ Date _____

Practice
For use with the lesson "Use Congruent Triangles"

Tell which triangles you can show are congruent in order to prove the statement. What postulate or theorem would you use?

1. $\overline{BC} \cong \overline{AD}$

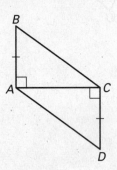

2. $\angle TSU \cong \angle VSU$

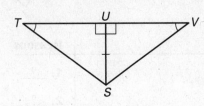

3. $\angle ADB \cong \angle CBD$

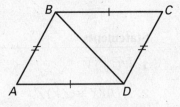

4. $\angle KHN \cong \angle MGT$

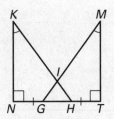

5. $\overline{BD} \cong \overline{BE}$

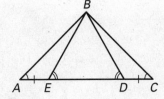

6. $\overline{BC} \cong \overline{AT}$

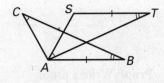

Use the diagram to write a plan for a proof.

7. PROVE: $\angle DAB \cong \angle BCD$

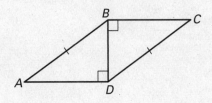

8. PROVE: $\overline{ST} \cong \overline{RQ}$

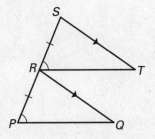

Name _____ Date _____

Use the vertices of △ABC and △DEF to show that ∠A ≅ ∠D.
***Explain* your reasoning.**

9. $A(1, 2)$, $B(4, -3)$, $C(2, 5)$, $D(4, 7)$, $E(7, 2)$, $F(5, 10)$

10. $A(2, 3)$, $B(2, 9)$, $C(6, 6)$, $D(8, 5)$, $E(8, 11)$, $F(12, 8)$

11. **Proof** Complete the proof.

GIVEN: $\overline{YX} \cong \overline{WX}$
$\overline{ZX}$ bisects ∠YXW.

PROVE: $\overline{YZ} \cong \overline{WZ}$

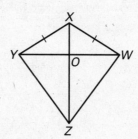

Statements	Reasons
1. $\overline{YX} \cong \overline{WX}$	**1.** ___?___
2. $\overline{ZX}$ bisects ∠YXW.	**2.** ___?___
3. ∠YXZ ≅ ∠WXZ	**3.** ___?___
4. $\overline{XZ} \cong \overline{XZ}$	**4.** ___?___
5. △YXZ ≅ △WXZ	**5.** ___?___
6. $\overline{YZ} \cong \overline{WZ}$	**6.** ___?___

Name _____   Date _____

Use the information given in the diagram to write a proof.

12. PROVE: $\overline{MN} \cong \overline{TQ}$

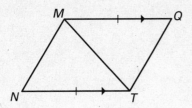

13. PROVE: $\overline{DB} \cong \overline{CB}$

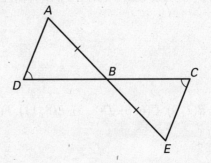

Name _____   Date _____

For use with the lesson "Use Isosceles and Equilateral Triangles"

Find the values of *x* and *y*.

1.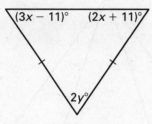

2.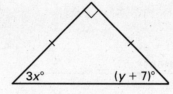

3.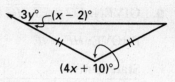

4.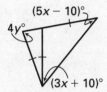

5.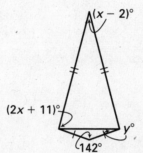

6.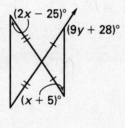

Decide whether enough information is given to prove that the triangles are congruent. *Explain* your answer.

7.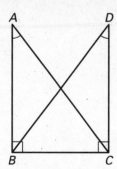

8.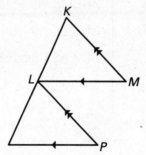

Name _____ Date _____

Practice *continued*
For use with the lesson "Use Isosceles and Equilateral Triangles"

In Exercises 9 and 10, complete the proof.

9. **GIVEN:** $\overline{FG} \cong \overline{FJ}, \overline{HG} \cong \overline{IJ}$

    PROVE: $\overline{HF} \cong \overline{IF}$

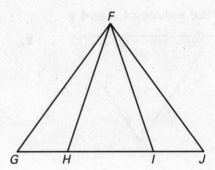

Statements	Reasons
1. $\overline{FG} \cong \overline{FJ}$	1. ?
2. ?	2. Base Angles Theorem
3. $\overline{HG} \cong \overline{IJ}$	3. ?
4. ?	4. SAS Congruence Postulate
5. $\overline{HF} \cong \overline{IF}$	5. ?

10. **GIVEN:** $\angle 1 \cong \angle 2, \overline{AC} \cong \overline{BD}$

    PROVE: $\angle 3 \cong \angle 4$

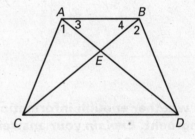

Statements	Reasons
1. $\angle 1 \cong \angle 2$	1. ?
2. $\overline{AC} \cong \overline{BD}$	2. ?
3. $\angle AEC \cong \angle BED$	3. ?
4. ?	4. AAS Congruence Theorem
5. $\overline{AE} \cong \overline{BE}$	5. ?
6. $\angle 3 \cong \angle 4$	6. ?

LESSON
4.8

Practice *continued*
For use with the lesson "Use Isosceles and Equilateral Triangles"

In Exercises 11–16, use the diagram. Complete the statement. Tell what theorem you used.

11. If $\overline{PQ} \cong \overline{PT}$, then $\angle$ __?__ $\cong \angle$ __?__.

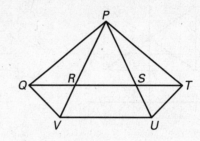

12. If $\angle PQV \cong \angle PVQ$, then __?__ $\cong$ __?__.

13. If $\overline{RP} \cong \overline{SP}$, then $\angle$ __?__ $\cong \angle$ __?__.

14. If $\overline{TP} \cong \overline{TR}$, then $\angle$ __?__ $\cong \angle$ __?__.

15. If $\angle PSQ \cong \angle SPQ$, then __?__ $\cong$ __?__.

16. If $\angle PUV \cong \angle PVU$, then __?__ $\cong$ __?__.

In Exercises 17–19, use the following information.

Prize Wheel A radio station sets up a prize wheel when they are out promoting their station. People spin the wheel and receive the prize that corresponds to the number the wheel stops on. The 9 triangles in the diagram are isosceles triangles with congruent vertex angles.

17. The measure of the vertex angle of triangle 1 is 40°. Find the measures of the base angles.

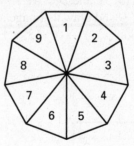

18. Explain how you know that triangle 1 is congruent to triangle 6.

19. Trace the prize wheel. Then form a triangle whose vertices are the midpoints of the bases of the triangles 1, 4, and 7. What type of triangle is this?

LESSON 4.9 Practice

For use with the lesson "Perform Congruence Transformations"

Name the type of transformation shown.

1.

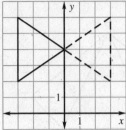

2.

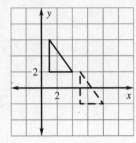

3.

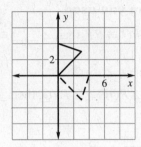

4. Figure *ABCD* has vertices *A*(1, 2), *B*(4, −3), *C*(5, 5), and *D*(4, 7). Sketch *ABCD* and draw its image after the translation $(x, y) \rightarrow (x + 5, y + 3)$.

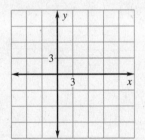

5. Figure *ABCD* has vertices *A*(−2, 3), *B*(1, 7), *C*(6, 2), and *D*(−1, −2). Sketch *ABCD* and draw its image after the translation $(x, y) \rightarrow (x - 2, y - 4)$.

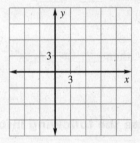

6. Figure *ABCD* has vertices *A*(3, −1), *B*(6, −2), *C*(5, 3), and *D*(0, 4). Sketch *ABCD* and draw its image after the translation $(x, y) \rightarrow (x - 3, y + 2)$.

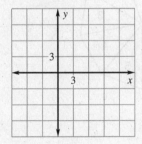

7. Figure *ABCD* has vertices *A*(−1, 3), *B*(4, −1), *C*(6, 4), and *D*(1, 5). Sketch *ABCD* and draw its image after the translation $(x, y) \rightarrow (x + 4, y - 5)$.

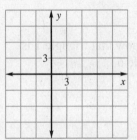

LESSON 4.9 **Practice** *continued*
For use with the lesson "Perform Congruence Transformations"

Use coordinate notation to describe the translation.

8. 3 units to the right, 5 units down

9. 7 units to the left, 2 units down

10. 4 units to the left, 6 units up

11. 1 unit to the right, 8 units up

Use a reflection in the *y*-axis to draw the other half of the figure.

12.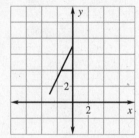

13.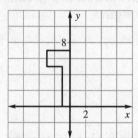

14.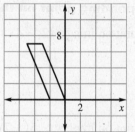

Use the coordinates to graph $\overline{AB}$ and $\overline{CD}$. Tell whether $\overline{CD}$ is a rotation of $\overline{AB}$ about the origin. If so, give the angle and direction of rotation.

15. $A(-2, 5)$, $B(-2, 0)$, $C(0, 1)$, $D(3, 1)$

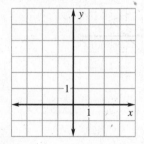

16. $A(1, 4)$, $B(4, 1)$, $C(1, -4)$, $D(4, -1)$

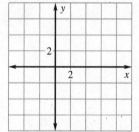

Name _____ Date _____

Complete the statement using the description of the translation. In the description, points (2, 0) and (3, 4) are two vertices of a triangle.

17. If $(2, 0)$ translates to $(4, 1)$, then $(3, 4)$ translates to __?__ .

18. If $(2, 0)$ translates to $(-2, -1)$, then $(3, 4)$ translates to __?__ .

A point on an image and the transformation are given. Find the corresponding point on the original figure.

19. Point on image: $(2, -4)$; transformation: $(x, y) \rightarrow (x - 4, y + 3)$

20. Point on image: $(-5, -7)$; transformation: $(x, y) \rightarrow (x, -y)$

21. **Verifying Congruence** Verify that
$\triangle DEF$ is a congruence transformation
of $\triangle ABC$. *Explain* your reasoning.

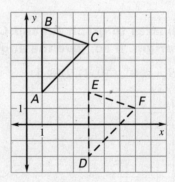

Name _____   Date _____

LESSON 5.1 **Practice**
For use with the lesson "Midsegment Theorem and Coordinate Proof"

$\overline{DE}$ **is a midsegment of** $\triangle ABC$. **Find the value of** *x*.

1.
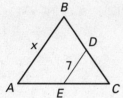

2.
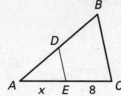

3.
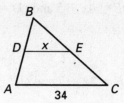

In $\triangle JKL$, $\overline{JR} \cong \overline{RK}$, $\overline{KS} \cong \overline{SL}$, **and** $\overline{JT} \cong \overline{TL}$. **Copy and complete the statement.**

4. $\overline{RS} \parallel$ ___?___

5. $\overline{ST} \parallel$ ___?___

6. $\overline{KL} \parallel$ ___?___

7. $\overline{SL} \cong$ ___?___ $\cong$ ___?___

8. $\overline{JR} \cong$ ___?___ $\cong$ ___?___

9. $\overline{JT} \cong$ ___?___ $\cong$ ___?___

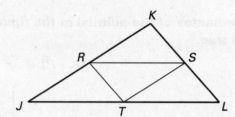

Place the figure in a coordinate plane in a convenient way. Assign coordinates to each vertex.

10. Right triangle: leg lengths are 5 units and 3 units

11. Rectangle: length is 7 units and width is 4 units

12. Square: side length is 6 units

13. Isosceles right triangle: leg length is 12 units

LESSON
5.1

Practice continued

For use with the lesson "Midsegment Theorem and Coordinate Proof"

Use △GHJ, where D, E, and F are midpoints of the sides.

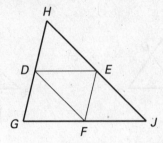

14. If $DE = 4x + 5$ and $GJ = 3x + 25$, what is DE?

15. If $EF = 2x + 7$ and $GH = 5x - 1$, what is EF?

16. If $HJ = 8x - 2$ and $DF = 2x + 11$, what is HJ?

Find the unknown coordinates of the point(s) in the figure. Then show that the given statement is true.

17. △$ABC \cong$ △DEC

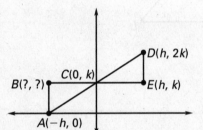

18. $\overline{PT} \cong \overline{SR}$

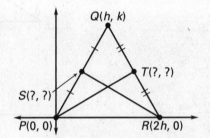

19. The coordinates of △ABC are $A(0, 5)$, $B(8, 20)$, and $C(0, 26)$. Find the length of each side and the perimeter of △ABC. Then find the perimeter of the triangle formed by connecting the three midsegments of △ABC.

LESSON 5.1

Practice *continued*
For use with the lesson "Midsegment Theorem and Coordinate Proof"

20. **Swing Set** You are assembling the frame for a swing set. The horizontal crossbars in the kit you purchased are each 36 inches long. You attach the crossbars at the midpoints of the legs. At each end of the frame, how far apart will the bottoms of the legs be when the frame is assembled? *Explain.*

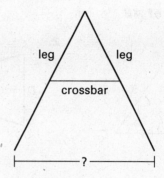

21. **A-Frame House** In an A-frame house, the floor of the second level, labeled $\overline{LM}$, is closer to the first floor, $\overline{NP}$, than is the midsegment $\overline{JK}$. If $\overline{JK}$ is 14 feet long, can $\overline{LM}$ be 12 feet long? 14 feet long? 20 feet long? 24 feet long? 30 feet long? *Explain.*

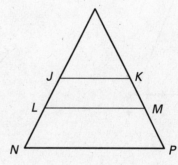

Name _____ Date _____

Practice
For use with the lesson "Use Perpendicular Bisectors"

Find the length of $\overline{AB}$.

1.

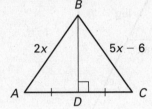

2.

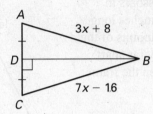

3.

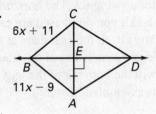

Tell whether the information in the diagram allows you to conclude that C is on the perpendicular bisector of $\overline{AB}$.

4.

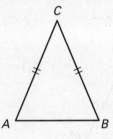

5.

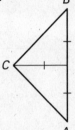

6.

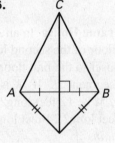

Use the diagram. $\overline{EH}$ is the perpendicular bisector of $\overline{DF}$. Find the indicated measure.

7. Find EF.

8. Find DE.

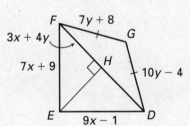

9. Find FG.

10. Find DG.

11. Find FH.

12. Find DF.

Name _____   Date _____

Practice *continued*

For use with the lesson "Use Perpendicular Bisectors"

In the diagram, the perpendicular bisectors of △ABC meet at point G and are shown dashed. Find the indicated measure.

13. Find AG.

14. Find BD.

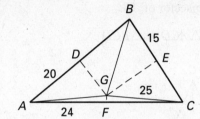

15. Find CF.

16. Find BG.

17. Find CE.

18. Find AC.

Draw $\overline{AB}$ with the given length. Construct the perpendicular bisector and choose point C on the perpendicular bisector so that the distance between C and $\overline{AB}$ is 1 inch. Measure $\overline{AC}$ and $\overline{BC}$.

19. $AB = 0.5$ inch

20. $AB = 1$ inch

21. $AB = 2$ inches

Name _____ Date _____

Write a two-column or a paragraph proof.

22. **GIVEN:** $\overline{CD}$ is the perpendicular bisector of $\overline{AB}$.

   PROVE: $\triangle ACD \cong \triangle BCD$

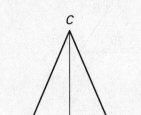

23. **GIVEN:** $\triangle GHJ \cong \triangle FHJ$

   PROVE: $\overline{EF} \cong \overline{EG}$

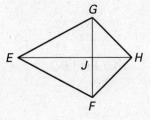

24. **Early Aircraft Set** On many of the earliest airplanes, wires connected vertical posts to the edges of the wings, which were wooden frames covered with cloth. The lengths of the wires from the top of a post to the edges of the frame are the same and distances from the bottom of the post to the ends of the two wires are the same. What does that tell you about the post and the section of frame between the ends of the wires?

Practice

LESSON 5.3

For use with the lesson "Use Angle Bisectors of Triangles"

Use the information in the diagram to find the measure.

1. Find *AD*.

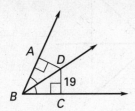

2. Find *m∠EFH*.

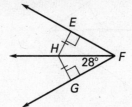

3. Find *m∠JKL*.

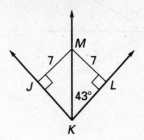

Can you conclude that $\overrightarrow{BD}$ **bisects** ∠*ABC*? ***Explain.***

4.

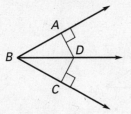

5.

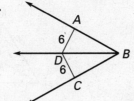

6.

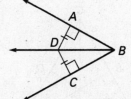

Find the value of *x*.

7.

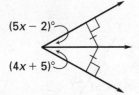

8.

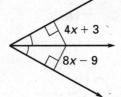

9.

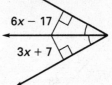

LESSON
5.3

Practice *continued*

For use with the lesson "Use Angle Bisectors of Triangles"

Can you find the value of *x*? **Explain.**

10.

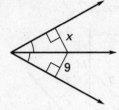

11.

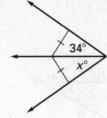

12.

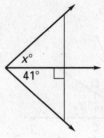

Find the indicated measure.

13. Point *G* is the incenter of △*ACE*.
Find *BG*.

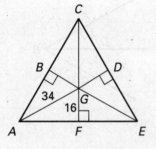

14. Point *P* is the incenter of △*HKM*.
Find *JP*.

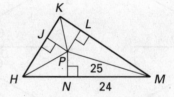

Find the value of *x* that makes *N* the incenter of the triangle.

15.

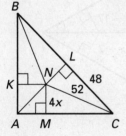

16.

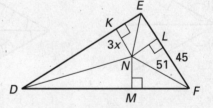

LESSON 5.3

Practice *continued*
For use with the lesson "Use Angle Bisectors of Triangles"

17. Hockey You and a friend are playing hockey in
your driveway. You are the goalie, and your
friend is going to shoot the puck from point *S*.
The goal extends from left goalpost *L* to right
goalpost *R*. Where should you position yourself
(point *G*) to have the best chance to prevent
your friend from scoring a goal? *Explain.*

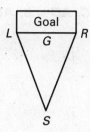

18. Monument You are building a monument in a triangular park. You want the
monument to be the same distance from each edge of the park. Use the figure with
incenter *G* to determine how far from point *D* you should build the monument.

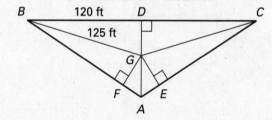

LESSON 5.4 **Practice**
For use with the lesson "Use Medians and Altitudes"

G is the centroid of △ABC, AD = 8, AG = 10, and CD = 18. Find the length of the segment.

1. $\overline{BD}$

2. $\overline{AB}$

3. $\overline{EG}$

4. $\overline{AE}$

5. $\overline{CG}$

6. $\overline{DG}$

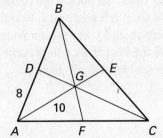

7. Use the graph shown.

   a. Find the coordinates of *M*, the midpoint of $\overline{JK}$.
   Use the median $\overline{LM}$ to find the coordinates
   of the centroid *P*.

   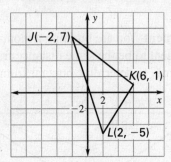

   b. Find the coordinates of *N*, the midpoint of $\overline{JL}$.
   Verify that $KP = \frac{2}{3}KN$.

Find the coordinates of the centroid P of △ABC.

8. $A(-7, -4), B(-3, 5), C(1, -4)$

9. $A(0, -2), B(6, 1), C(9, -5)$

Is $\overline{BD}$ a *perpendicular bisector* of △ABC? Is $\overline{BD}$ a *median*? an *altitude*?

10.
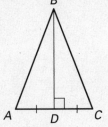

11.
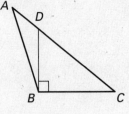

12.
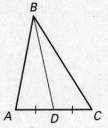

**LESSON
5.4** **Practice** *continued*
For use with the lesson "Use Medians and Altitudes"

Find the measurements.

13. Given that $AB = BC$, find AD and $m\angle ABC$.

14. Given that G is the centroid of $\triangle ABC$, find FG and BD.

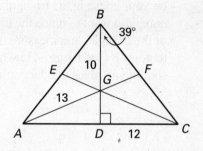

Copy and complete the statement for $\triangle HJK$ with medians $\overline{HN}$, $\overline{JL}$, and $\overline{KM}$, and centroid P.

15. $PN = \underline{\ ?\ } HN$

16. $PL = \underline{\ ?\ } JP$

17. $KP = \underline{\ ?\ } KM$

Point G is the centroid of $\triangle ABC$. Use the given information to find the value of x.

18. $CG = 3x + 7$ and $CE = 6x$

19. $FG = x + 8$ and $AF = 9x - 6$

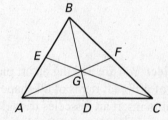

20. $BG = 5x - 1$ and $DG = 4x - 5$

Complete the sentence with *always, sometimes,* or *never*.

21. The median of a triangle is __?__ the perpendicular bisector.

22. The altitude of a triangle is __?__ the perpendicular bisector.

23. The medians of a triangle __?__ intersect inside the triangle.

24. The altitudes of a triangle __?__ intersect inside the triangle.

LESSON 5.4	**Practice** *continued*
	For use with the lesson "Use Medians and Altitudes"

25. House Decoration You are going to put a decoration on your house in the triangular area above the front door. You want to place the decoration on the centroid of the triangle. You measure the distance from point *A* to point *B* (see figure). How far down from point *A* should you place the decoration? *Explain*.

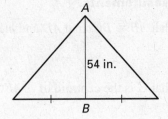

54 in.

26. Art Project You are making an art piece which consists of different items of all shapes and sizes. You want to insert an isosceles triangle with the dimensions shown. In order for the triangle to fit, the height (altitude) must be less than 8.5 millimeters. Find the altitude. Will the triangle fit in your art piece?

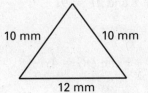

10 mm   10 mm

12 mm

Name _____   Date _____

Practice
For use with the lesson "Use Inequalities in a Triangle"

Use a ruler and protractor to draw the given type of triangle. Mark the largest angle and longest side in red and the smallest angle and shortest side in blue. What do you notice?

1. Obtuse scalene

2. Acute isosceles

3. Right isosceles

List the sides and the angles in order from smallest to largest.

4.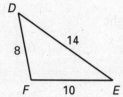

5.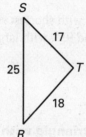

6.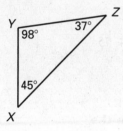

7.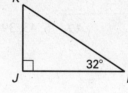

8.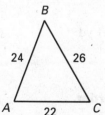

9.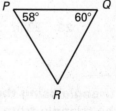

Name _____ Date _____

Sketch and label the triangle described.

10. Side lengths: 14, 17, and 19, with longest side on the bottom
Angle measures: 45°, 60°, and 75°, with smallest angle at the right

11. Side lengths: 11, 18, and 24, with shortest side on the bottom
Angle measures: 25°, 44°, and 111°, with largest angle at the left

12. Side lengths: 32, 34, and 48, with shortest side arranged vertically at the right.
Angle measures: 42°, 45°, and 93°, with largest angle at the top.

Is it possible to construct a triangle with the given side lengths? If not,
***explain* why not.**

13. 3, 4, 5   14. 1, 4, 6   15. 17, 17, 33

16. 22, 26, 65   17. 6, 43, 39   18. 7, 54, 45

***Describe* the possible lengths of the third side of the triangle given the**
lengths of the other two sides.

19. 6 in., 9 in.   20. 4 ft, 12 ft   21. 9 m, 18 m

22. 21 yd, 16 yd   23. 22 in., 2 ft   24. 24 in., 1 yd

Is it possible to build a triangle using the given side lengths? If so, order
the angle measures of the triangle from least to greatest.

25. $RS = \sqrt{46}, ST = 3\sqrt{5}, RT = 5$ 26. $AB = \sqrt{26}, BC = 4\sqrt{5}, AC = 2\sqrt{2}$

Name _____ Date _____

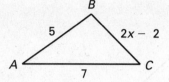
Describe the possible values of x.

27.

B
5   2x − 2
A ———————— C
        7

28.

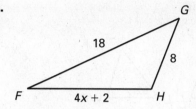

29. **Building** You are standing 200 feet from a tall
building. The angle of elevation from your feet to the
top of the building is 51° (as shown in the figure).
What can you say about the height of the building?

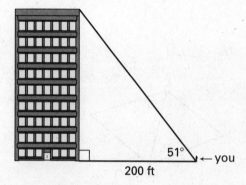

30. **Sea Rescue** The figure shows the relative
positions of two rescue boats and two people
in the water. Talking by radio, the captains use
certain angle relationships to conclude that
boat *A* is the closest to person *C* and boat *B* is
the closest to person *D*. *Describe* the angle
relationships that would lead to this conclusion.

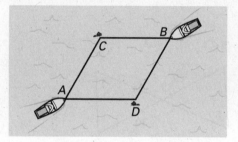

31. **Airplanes** Two airplanes leave the same airport heading in different directions.
After 2 hours, one airplane has traveled 710 miles and the other has traveled
640 miles. *Describe* the range of distances that represents how far apart the
two airplanes can be at this time.

32. **Baseball** A pitcher throws a baseball 60 feet from the pitcher's mound to home
plate. A batter pops the ball up and it comes down just 24 feet from home plate.
What can you determine about how far the ball lands from pitcher's mound?
Explain why the Triangle Inequality Theorem can be used to describe all but
the shortest and longest possible distances.

Name _____ Date _____

Practice

For use with the lesson "Inequalities in Two Triangles and Indirect Proof"

Complete with <, >, or = . *Explain.*

1. ST __?__ VW

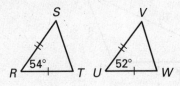

2. DE __?__ EF

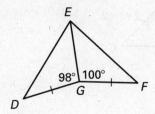

3. JK __?__ LM

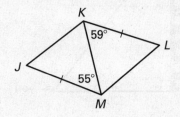

4. $m\angle 1$ __?__ $m\angle 2$

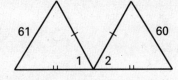

5. $m\angle 1$ __?__ $m\angle 2$

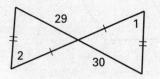

6. $m\angle 1$ __?__ $m\angle 2$

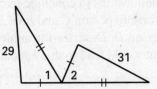

7. $m\angle 1$ __?__ $m\angle 2$

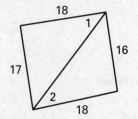

8. AB __?__ CD

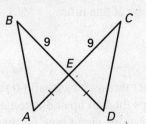

**LESSON
5.6**

Practice *continued*
For use with the lesson "Inequalities in Two Triangles and Indirect Proof"

Use the Hinge Theorem or its converse and properties of triangles to write and solve an inequality to describe a restriction on the value of *x*.

9.

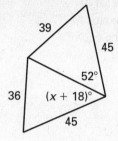

10.

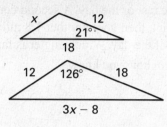

Write a temporary assumption you could make to prove the conclusion indirectly.

11. If two lines in a plane are parallel, then the two lines do not contain two sides of a triangle.

12. If two parallel lines are cut by a transversal so that a pair of consecutive interior angles is congruent, then the transversal is perpendicular to the parallel lines.

13. **Table Making** All four legs of the table shown have identical measurements, but they are attached to the table top so that the measure of $\angle 3$ is smaller than the measure of $\angle 1$.

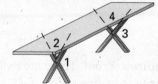

a. Use the Hinge Theorem to *explain* why the table top is not level.

b. Use the Converse of the Hinge Theorem to *explain* how to use a length measure to determine when $\angle 4 \cong \angle 2$ in reattaching the rear pair of legs to make the table level.

LESSON 5.6 **Practice** *continued*
For use with the lesson "Inequalities in Two Triangles and Indirect Proof"

14. Fishing Contest One contestant in a catch-and-release fishing contest spends the morning at a location 1.8 miles due north of the starting point, then goes 1.2 miles due east for the rest of the day. A second contestant starts out 1.2 miles due east of the starting point, then goes another 1.8 miles in a direction 84° south of due east to spend the rest of the day. Which angler is farther from the starting point at the end of the day? *Explain* how you know.

15. Indirect Proof Arrange statements A–F in order to write an indirect proof of Case 1.

GIVEN: $\overline{AD}$ is a median of $\triangle ABC$.
   $\angle ADB \cong \angle ADC$

PROVE: $AB = AC$

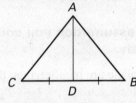

Case 1:

A. Then $m\angle ADB < m\angle ADC$ by the converse of the Hinge Theorem.

B. Then $\overline{BD} \cong \overline{CD}$ by the definition of midpoint. Also, $\overline{AD} \cong \overline{AD}$ by the reflexive property.

C. This contradiction shows that the temporary assumption that $AB < AC$ is false.

D. But this contradicts the given statement that $\angle ADB \cong \angle ADC$.

E. Because $\overline{AD}$ is a median of $\triangle ABC$, D is the midpoint of $\overline{BC}$.

F. Temporarily assume that $AB < AC$.

16. Indirect Proof There are two cases to consider for the proof in Exercise 15. Write an indirect proof for Case 2.

Name _____ Date _____

List all pairs of congruent angles for the figures. Then write the ratios of the corresponding sides in a statement of proportionality.

1. $\triangle ABC \sim \triangle DFE$

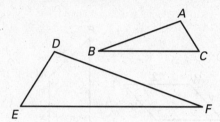

2. $WXYZ \sim MNOP$

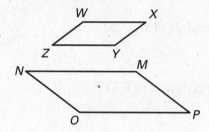

3. **Multiple Choice** Triangles ABC and DEF are similar. Which statement is not correct?

A. $\dfrac{AB}{DE} = \dfrac{BC}{EF}$

B. $\dfrac{CA}{FD} = \dfrac{AB}{DE}$

C. $\angle A \cong \angle F$

Determine whether the polygons are similar. If they are, write a similarity statement and find the scale factor.

4.

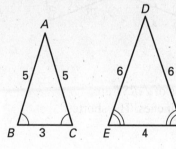

5.

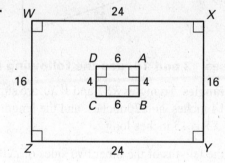

LESSON 6.1

Practice *continued*
For use with the lesson "Use Similar Polygons"

In the diagram, *WXYZ* ~ *MNOP*.

6. Find the scale factor of *WXYZ* to *MNOP*.

7. Find the values of *x*, *y*, and *z*.

8. Find the perimeter of *WXYZ*.

9. Find the perimeter of *MNOP*.

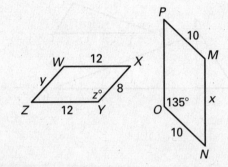

10. Find the ratio of the perimeter of *MNOP* to the perimeter of *WXYZ*.

The two triangles are similar. Find the values of the variables.

11.

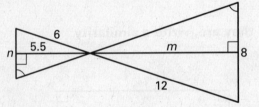

12.

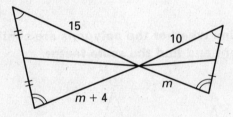

In Exercises 13 and 14, use the following information.

Similar Triangles Triangles *RST* and *WXY* are similar. The side lengths of $\triangle RST$ are 10 inches, 14 inches, and 20 inches, and the length of an altitude is 6.5 inches. The shortest side of $\triangle WXY$ is 15 inches long.

13. Find the lengths of the other two sides of $\triangle WXY$.

14. Find the length of the corresponding altitude in $\triangle WXY$.

15. **Multiple Choice** The ratio of one side of $\triangle ABC$ to the corresponding side of a similar $\triangle DEF$ is 4 : 3. The perimeter of $\triangle DEF$ is 24 inches. What is the perimeter of $\triangle ABC$?

   A. 18 inches   **B.** 24 inches   **C.** 32 inches

Practice continued
For use with the lesson "Use Similar Polygons"

In the diagram, △XYZ ~ △MNP.

16. Find the scale factor of △XYZ to △MNP.

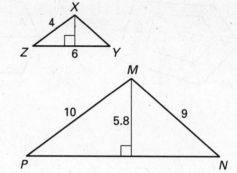

17. Find the unknown side lengths of both triangles.

18. Find the length of the altitude shown in △XYZ.

19. Find and compare the areas of both triangles.

In Exercises 20–22, use the following information.

Swimming Pool The community park has a rectangular swimming pool enclosed by a rectangular fence for sunbathing. The shape of the pool is similar to the shape of the fence. The pool is 30 feet wide. The fence is 50 feet wide and 100 feet long.

20. What is the scale factor of the pool to the fence?

21. What is the length of the pool?

22. Find the area reserved strictly for sunbathing.

Name _____ Date _____

Practice

For use with the lesson "Transformations and Similarity"

Describe the dilation that moves figure A onto figure B.

1.
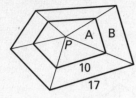

2.
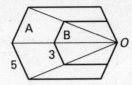

3.
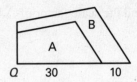

The two figures are similar. Describe the transformation(s) that move figure A onto figure B.

4.
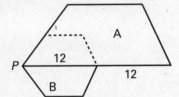

5.
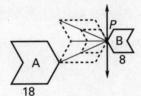

6.
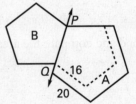

Draw an example of the given similarity transformation of the figure with center O.

7. dilation
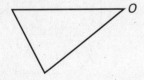

8. dilation then translation
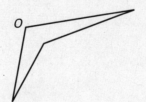

9. dilation then rotation

LESSON
6.2

Practice *continued*
For use with the lesson "Transformations and Similarity"

Figure B is the image of figure A under a transformation. Tell whether the transformation involves a dilation. If so, give the scale factor of the dilation.

10.

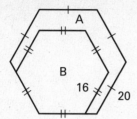

11.

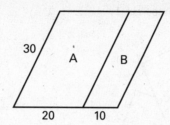

12.

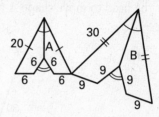

Coordinates of the vertices of a preimage and image figure are given. Describe the transformations that move the first figure onto the second.

13. $A(-4, 2)$, $B(2, 4)$, $C(-2, 5)$; $P(-8, 4)$, $Q(4, 8)$, $R(-4, 10)$

14. $O(0, 0)$, $M(0, 4)$, $N(6, 0)$; $O(0, 0)$, $F(0, 10)$, $G(15, 0)$

15. $O(0, 0)$, $S(0, 2)$, $T(5, 0)$; $O(0, 0)$, $X(0, -4)$, $Y(-10, 0)$

16. $A(-8, 0)$, $B(0, -10)$, $O(0, 0)$; $P(4, 0)$, $Q(0, 5)$, $O(0, 0)$

17. $J(-16, 0)$, $K(0, -20)$, $O(0, 0)$; $M(-8, 0)$, $N(0, 10)$, $O(0, 0)$

LESSON 6.2

Practice *continued*

For use with the lesson "Transformations and Similarity"

18. **Crafts** Gail cuts and glues similar shapes onto a wooden board as a crafts project. One design with similar shapes is shown at the right. Describe a combination of three transformations that can be used to move shape A onto shape B.

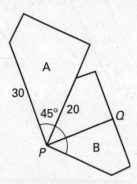

19. **Computers** Cameron uses graphics software to create the figure shown at the right. He wants the length of the smaller flower petals to be $\frac{3}{5}$ of the length of the larger petals. Describe a combination of transformations that can be used to move petal A onto petal B.

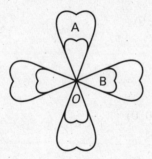

Circle B is the image of circle A under a transformation. Prove the circles are similar by finding a center and scale factor of a dilation that moves circle *A* onto circle *B*.

20. tangent

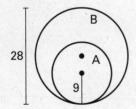

21. concentric

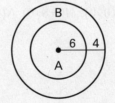

LESSON 6.3 Practice

For use with the lesson "Prove Triangles Similar by AA"

Use the diagram to complete the statement.

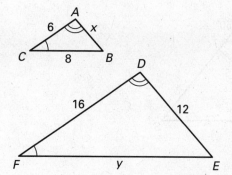

1. $\triangle ABC \sim$ ___?___

2. $\dfrac{AB}{?} = \dfrac{?}{EF} = \dfrac{CA}{?}$

3. $\angle B \cong$ ___?___

4. $\dfrac{?}{12} = \dfrac{8}{?}$

5. $x =$ ___?___

6. $y =$ ___?___

Determine whether the triangles are similar. If they are, write a similarity statement.

7.
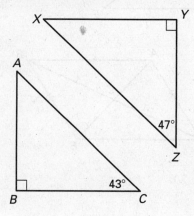

8.
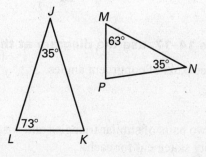

9.
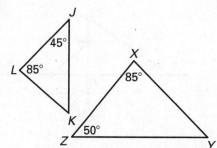

10.
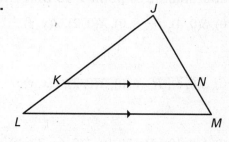

Practice *continued*
For use with the lesson "Prove Triangles Similar by AA"

11.

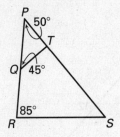

12.

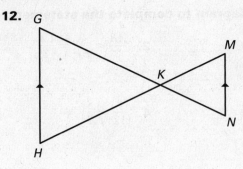

13. **Multiple Choice** In the diagram at the right, find the length of $\overline{BC}$.

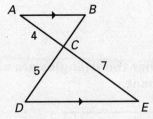

A. $\dfrac{28}{5}$ **B.** 6

C. 3 **D.** $\dfrac{20}{7}$

In Exercises 14–17, use the diagram at the right.

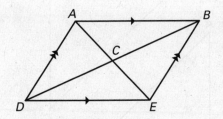

14. List three pairs of congruent angles.

15. Name two pairs of similar triangles and write a similarity statement for each.

16. Is $\triangle ACD \sim \triangle BCE$?

17. Is $\triangle AED \cong \triangle EAB$?

In Exercises 18–21, use the diagram at the right.
Find the coordinates of point Z so that $\triangle RST \sim \triangle RXZ$.

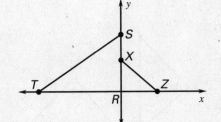

18. $R(0, 0)$, $S(0, 4)$, $T(-8, 0)$, $X(0, 2)$, $Z(x, y)$

19. $R(0, 0)$, $S(0, 6)$, $T(-6, 0)$, $X(0, 2)$, $Z(x, y)$

20. $R(0, 0)$, $S(0, 10)$, $T(-20, 0)$, $X(0, 6)$, $Z(x, y)$

21. $R(0, 0)$, $S(0, 7)$, $T(-9, 0)$, $X(0, 4)$, $Z(x, y)$

Practice *continued*
For use with the lesson "Prove Triangles Similar by AA"

22. Multiple Choice Triangles *ABC* and *DEF* are right triangles that are similar.
$\overline{AB}$ and $\overline{BC}$ are the legs of the first triangle. $\overline{DE}$ and $\overline{EF}$ are the legs of the second
triangle. Which of the following is false?

A. $\angle A \cong \angle D$ **B.** $AC = DF$ **C.** $\dfrac{AC}{DF} = \dfrac{AB}{DE}$

In Exercises 23–25, use the following information.

Flag Pole In order to estimate the height *h* of a flag
pole, a 5 foot tall male student stands so that the tip
of his shadow coincides with the tip of the flag pole's
shadow. This scenario results in two similar triangles
as shown in the diagram.

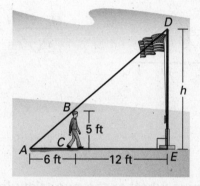

23. Why are the two overlapping triangles similar?

24. Using the similar triangles, write a proportion
that models the situation.

25. What is the height *h* (in feet) of the flag pole?

Name _____ Date _____

Practice

For use with the lesson "Prove Triangles Similar by SSS and SAS"

Is either △LMN or △RST similar to △ABC?

1.

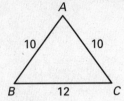

2.

Determine whether the two triangles are similar. If they are similar, write a similarity statement and find the scale factor of △A to △B.

3.

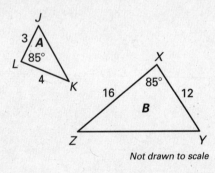

Not drawn to scale

4.

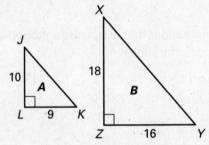

5. Algebra Find the value of m that makes $\triangle ABC \sim \triangle DEF$ when $AB = 3$, $BC = 4$, $DE = 2m$, $EF = m + 5$, and $\angle B \cong \angle E$.

Name _____   Date _____

Show that the triangles are similar and write a similarity statement.
***Explain* your reasoning.**

6.
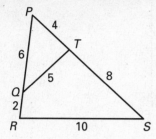

7.
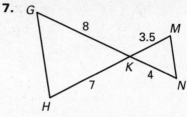

8. **Multiple Choice** In the diagram at the right, △ACE ~ △DCB. Find the length of $\overline{AB}$.

A. 12

B. 18

C. $\frac{35}{2}$

D. $\frac{30}{7}$

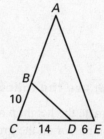

Sketch the triangles using the given description. *Explain* whether the two triangles can be similar.

9. The side lengths of △ABC are 8, 10 and 14.

The side lengths of △DEF are 16, 20 and 26.

10. In △ABC, AB = 15, BC = 24 and $m\angle B = 38°$.

In △DEF, DE = 5, EF = 8 and $m\angle E = 38°$.

Name _____ Date _____

Practice continued

For use with the lesson "Prove Triangles Similar by SSS and SAS"

In Exercises 11–14, use the diagram at the right to copy and complete the statement.

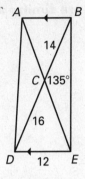

11. $\triangle ABC \sim$ ___?___

12. $m\angle DCE =$ ___?___

13. $AB =$ ___?___

14. $m\angle CAB + m\angle ABC =$ ___?___

In Exercises 15 and 16, use the following information.

Pine Tree In order to estimate the height h of a tall pine tree, a student places a mirror on the ground and stands where she can see the top of the tree, as shown. The student is 6 feet tall and stands 3 feet from the mirror which is 11 feet from the base of the tree.

15. What is the height h (in feet) of the pine tree?

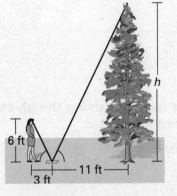

16. Another student also wants to see the top of the tree. The other student is 5.5 feet tall. If the mirror is to remain 3 feet from the student's feet, how far from the base of the tree should the mirror be placed?

Name _____ Date _____

6.5
Practice
For use with the lesson "Use Proportionality Theorems"

Use the figure to complete the proportion.

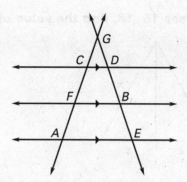

1. $\dfrac{GC}{CF} = \dfrac{?}{DB}$

2. $\dfrac{AF}{FC} = \dfrac{?}{BD}$

3. $\dfrac{CD}{FB} = \dfrac{GD}{?}$

4. $\dfrac{AE}{CD} = \dfrac{GE}{?}$

5. $\dfrac{FG}{AG} = \dfrac{FB}{?}$

6. $\dfrac{GD}{GE} = \dfrac{?}{AE}$

Use the given information to determine whether $\overline{BD} \parallel \overline{AE}$.

7.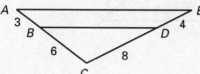

8.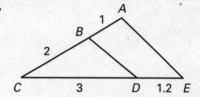

9.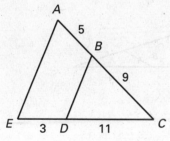

10.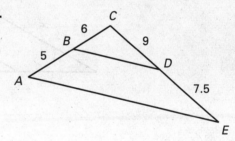

Determine the length of each segment.

11. $\overline{BC}$

12. $\overline{FC}$

13. $\overline{GB}$

14. $\overline{CD}$

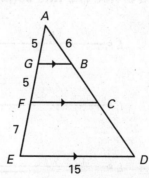

Copyright © Houghton Mifflin Harcourt Publishing Company. All rights reserved.

Geometry
Practice Workbook   **115**

LESSON
6.5

Practice   continued
For use with the lesson "Use Proportionality Theorems"

In Exercises 15–18, find the value of x.

15.

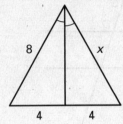

16.

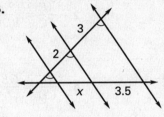

17.

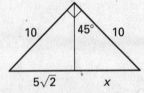

18.

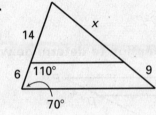

Find the value of the variable.

19. *x*

20. *m*

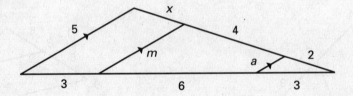

21. *a*

Use construction tools to divide the line segment into the given number of equal parts.

22. 4

L ●━━━━━━━━━━━━━━━━━━━━● M

23. 3

L ●━━━━━━━━━━━━━━━━━━━━● M

24. 2

L ●━━━━━━━━━━━━━━━━━━● M

LESSON
6.5

Practice continued
For use with the lesson "Use Proportionality Theorems"

25. **Maps** On the map below, 51st Street and 52nd Street are parallel. Charlie walks from point A to point B and then from point B to point C. You walk directly from point A to point C.

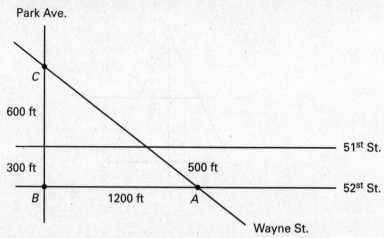

a. How many more feet did Charlie walk than you?

b. Park Avenue is perpendicular to 51st Street. Is Park Avenue perpendicular to 52nd Street? *Explain.*

Name _____ Date _____

Practice

For use with the lesson "Perform Similarity Transformations"

Draw a dilation of the figure using the given scale factor.

1. $k = 2$

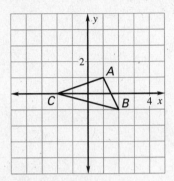

2. $k = \frac{1}{4}$

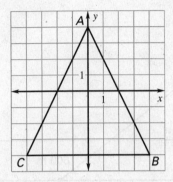

3. $k = \frac{1}{2}$

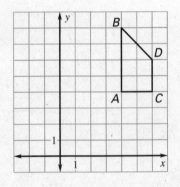

4. $k = 1\frac{1}{2}$

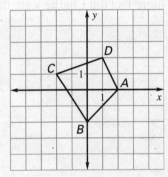

Determine whether the dilation from Figure A to Figure B is a *reduction* or an *enlargement*. Then, find the values of the variables.

5.

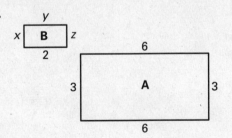

6.

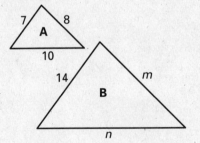

LESSON 6.6 **Practice** *continued*
For use with the lesson "Perform Similarity Transformations"

7.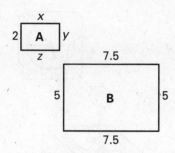

8.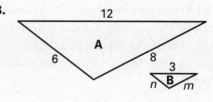

Determine whether the transformation from Figure A to Figure B is a translation, reflection, rotation, or dilation.

9.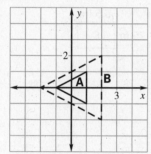

10.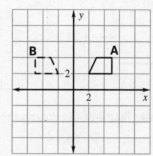

11.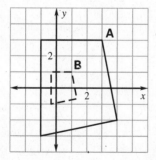

12.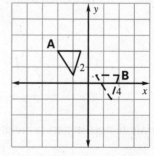

LESSON
6.6

Practice *continued*

For use with the lesson "Perform Similarity Transformations"

13. Overhead Projectors Your teacher draws a circle on an overhead projector. The projector then displays an enlargement of the circle on the wall. The circle drawn has a radius of 3 inches. The circle on the wall has a diameter of 4 feet. What is the scale factor of the enlargement?

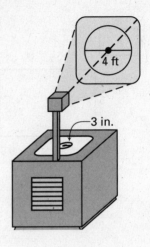

14. Posters A poster is enlarged and then the enlargement is reduced as shown in the figure.

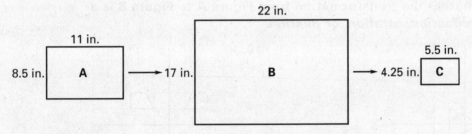

a. What is the scale factor of the enlargement? the reduction?

b. A second poster is reduced directly from size A to size C. What is the scale factor of the reduction?

c. How are the scale factors in part (a) related to the scale factor in part (b)?

Name _____ Date _____

Practice
For use with the lesson "Apply the Pythagorean Theorem"

Use △ABC to determine if the equation is *true* or *false*.

1. $b^2 + a^2 = c^2$

2. $c^2 - a^2 = b^2$

3. $b^2 - c^2 = a^2$

4. $c^2 = a^2 - b^2$

5. $c^2 = b^2 + a^2$

6. $a^2 = c^2 - b^2$

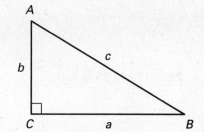

**Find the unknown side length. Simplify answers that are radicals.
Tell whether the side lengths form a Pythagorean triple.**

7.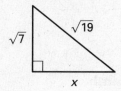

8.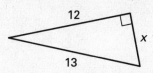

9.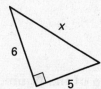

10.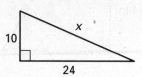

11.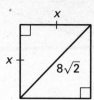

12.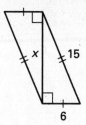

**The given lengths are two sides of a right triangle. All three side lengths
of the triangle are integers and together form a Pythagorean triple. Find
the length of the third side and tell whether it is a leg or the hypotenuse.**

13. 40 and 41

14. 12 and 35

15. 63 and 65

LESSON 7.1 | **Practice** *continued*
For use with the lesson "Apply the Pythagorean Theorem"

16. 28 and 45

17. 56 and 65

18. 20 and 29

19. 80 and 89

20. 48 and 55

21. 65 and 72

Find the area of a right triangle with given leg ℓ and hypotenuse h. Round decimal answers to the nearest tenth.

22. $\ell = 8$ m, $h = 16$ m

23. $\ell = 9$ yd, $h = 12$ yd

24. $\ell = 3.5$ ft, $h = 9$ ft

25. $\ell = 9$ mi, $h = 10$ mi

26. $\ell = 21$ in., $h = 29$ in.

27. $\ell = 13$ cm, $h = 17$ cm

Find the area of the figure. Round decimal answers to the nearest tenth.

28.
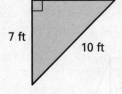
7 ft
10 ft

29.
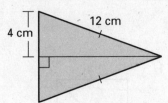
4 cm
12 cm

30.
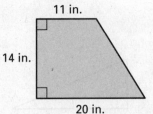
11 in.
14 in.
20 in.

31.
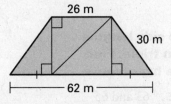
26 m
30 m
62 m

32.
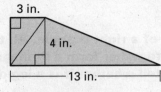
3 in.
4 in.
13 in.

33.
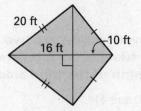
20 ft
10 ft
16 ft

Name _____ Date _____

Practice *continued*
For use with the lesson "Apply the Pythagorean Theorem"

34. Softball In slow-pitch softball, the distance of the paths between each pair of
consecutive bases is 65 feet and the paths form right angles. Find the distance the
catcher must throw a softball from 3 feet behind home plate to second base.

35. Flight Distance A small commuter airline
flies to three cities whose locations form the
vertices of a right triangle. The total flight
distance (from city A to city B to city C and
back to city A) is 1400 miles. It is 600 miles
between the two cities that are furthest apart.
Find the other two distances between cities.

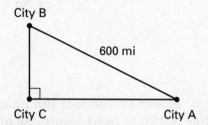

In Exercises 36–38, use the following information.

Garden You have a garden that is in the shape of a right triangle with the dimensions shown.

36. Find the perimeter of the garden.

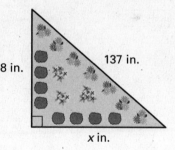

37. You are going to plant a post every
15 inches around the garden's perimeter.
How many posts do you need?

38. You plan to attach fencing to the posts
to enclose the garden. If each post costs
$1.25 and each foot of fencing costs $.70,
how much will it cost to enclose the
garden? *Explain*.

Name _____ Date _____

Decide whether the numbers can represent the side lengths of a triangle. If they can, classify the triangle as *right, acute,* or *obtuse*.

1. 5, 12, 13

2. $\sqrt{8}$, 4, 6

3. 20, 21, 28

4. 15, 36, 39

5. $\sqrt{13}$, 10, 12

6. 14, 48, 50

Graph points *A, B,* and *C*. Connect the points to form △*ABC*. Decide whether △*ABC* is *right, acute,* or *obtuse*.

7. $A(-3, 5)$, $B(0, -2)$, $C(4, 1)$

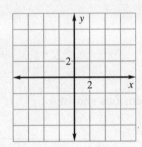

8. $A(-8, -4)$, $B(-5, -2)$, $C(-1, -7)$

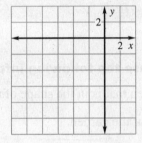

9. $A(4, 1)$, $B(7, -2)$, $C(2, -4)$

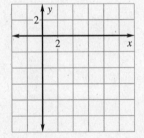

10. $A(-2, 2)$, $B(6, 4)$, $C(-4, 10)$

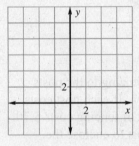

LESSON 7.2

Practice *continued*
For use with the lesson "Use the Converse of the Pythagorean Theorem"

11. $A(0, 5)$, $B(3, 6)$, $C(5, 1)$

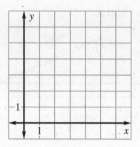

12. $A(-2, 4)$, $B(2, 0)$, $C(5, 2)$

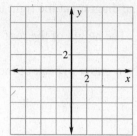

In Exercises 13 and 14, copy and complete the statement with <, >, or = , if possible. If it is not possible, *explain* why.

13. $m\angle J$ __?__ $m\angle R$

14. $m\angle K + m\angle L$ __?__ $m\angle S + m\angle T$

The sides and classification of a triangle are given below. The length of the longest side is the integer given. What value(s) of *x* make the triangle?

15. $x, x, 8$; right

16. $x, x, 12$; obtuse

17. $x, x, 6$; acute

18. $x, x + 3, 15$; obtuse

19. $x, x - 8, 40$; right

20. $x + 2, x + 3, 29$; acute

Name _____ Date _____

Practice *continued*
For use with the lesson "Use the Converse of the Pythagorean Theorem"

In Exercises 21 and 22, use the diagram and the following information.

Roof The roof shown in the diagram at the right is shown from the front of the house.

The slope of the roof is $\frac{5}{12}$. The height of the roof is 15 feet.

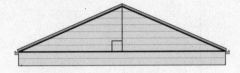

21. What is the length from gutter to peak of the roof?

22. A row of shingles is 5 inches high. How many rows of shingles are needed for one side of the roof?

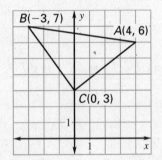
Shingle
5 in.

In Exercises 23–25, you will use two different methods for determining whether △ ABC is a right triangle.

23. **Method 1** Find the slope of $\overline{AC}$ and the slope of $\overline{BC}$. What do the slopes tell you about $\angle ACB$? Is $\triangle ABC$ a right triangle? How do you know?

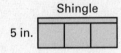

B(−3, 7)   y

A(4, 6)

C(0, 3)

1

1   x

24. **Method 2** Use the Distance Formula and the Converse of the Pythagorean Theorem to determine whether $\triangle ABC$ is a right triangle.

25. **Compare** Which method would you use to determine whether a given triangle is right, acute, or obtuse? *Explain.*

Name _____   Date _____

LESSON 7.3 Practice
For use with the lesson "Use Similar Right Triangles"

Complete and solve the proportion.

1. $\dfrac{x}{12} = \dfrac{?}{8}$

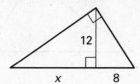

2. $\dfrac{15}{x} = \dfrac{x}{?}$

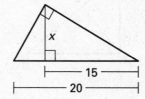

3. $\dfrac{9}{x} = \dfrac{x}{?}$

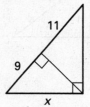

Find the value(s) of the variable(s).

4.

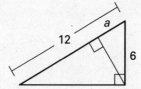

5.

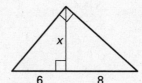

6.

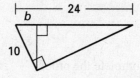

7.

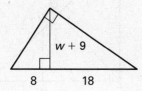

8.

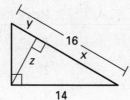

9.

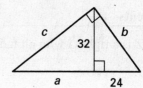

Tell whether the triangle is a right triangle. If so, find the length of the altitude to the hypotenuse. Round decimal answers to the nearest tenth.

10.

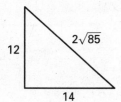

11.

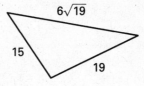

12.

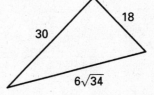

**LESSON
7.3** **Practice** *continued*
For use with the lesson "Use Similar Right Triangles"

Use the Geometric Mean Theorems to find *AC* and *BD*.

13.

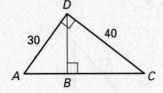

14.

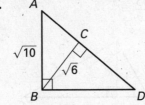

15.

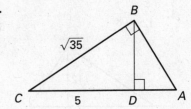

16. Complete the proof.

GIVEN: $\triangle XYZ$ is a right triangle with $m\angle XYZ = 90°$.
$\overline{VW} \parallel \overline{XY}$, $\overline{YU}$ is an altitude of $\triangle XYZ$.

PROVE: $\triangle YUZ \sim \triangle VWZ$

Statements	Reasons
1. $\triangle XYZ$ is a right $\triangle$ with altitude $\overline{YU}$.	1. ___?___
2. $\triangle XYZ \sim \triangle YUZ$	2. ___?___
3. $\overline{VW} \parallel \overline{XY}$	3. ___?___
4. $\angle VWZ \cong \angle XYZ$	4. ___?___
5. $\angle Z \cong \angle Z$	5. ___?___
6. ___?___	6. AA Similarity Postulate
7. $\triangle YUZ \sim \triangle VWZ$	7. ___?___

LESSON 7.3 **Practice** *continued*
For use with the lesson "Use Similar Right Triangles"

In Exercises 17–19, use the diagram.

17. Sketch the three similar triangles in the diagram.
    Label the vertices.

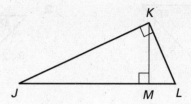

18. Write similarity statements for the three triangles.

19. Which segment's length is the geometric mean of
    LM and *JM*?

20. **Kite Design** You are designing a diamond-shaped
    kite. You know that $AB = 38.4$ centimeters,
    $BC = 72$ centimeters, and $AC = 81.6$ centimeters.
    You want to use a straight crossbar $\overline{BD}$. About how
    long should it be?

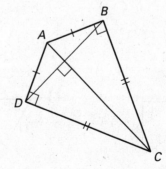

LESSON 7.4 **Practice**
For use with the lesson "Special Right Triangles"

Find the value of x. Write your answer in simplest radical form.

1.

2.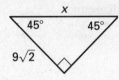

3.

4.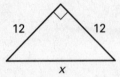

5.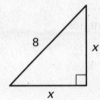

6.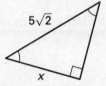

Find the value of each variable. Write your answers in simplest radical form.

7.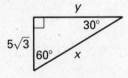

8.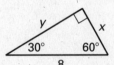

9.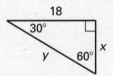

10.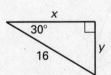

11.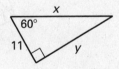

12.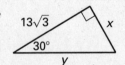

Name _____   Date _____

Practice *continued*
For use with the lesson "Special Right Triangles"

Complete the table.

13.

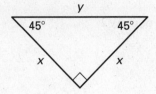

x	5		$\sqrt{2}$	9	
y		$4\sqrt{2}$			24

14.

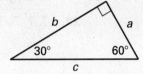

a	9			11	
b		9	$5\sqrt{3}$		
c					16

Find the value of each variable. Write your answers in simplest radical form.

15.

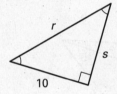

16.

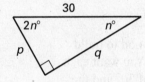

17.

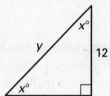

18.

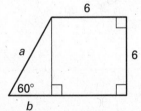

19.

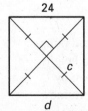

20.

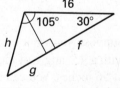

Practice *continued*
For use with the lesson "Special Right Triangles"

**The side lengths of a triangle are given. Determine whether it is a
45°-45°-90° triangle, a 30°-60°-90° triangle, or neither.**

21. $5, 10, 5\sqrt{3}$ **22.** $7, 7, 7\sqrt{3}$ **23.** $6, 6, 6\sqrt{2}$

24. Roofing You are replacing the roof on the
house shown, and you want to know the total
area of the roof. The roof has a 1-1 pitch on
both sides, which means that it slopes upward
at a rate of 1 vertical unit for each 1 horizontal unit.

   a. Find the values of x and y in the diagram.

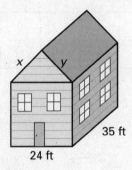

   b. Find the total area of the roof to the nearest square foot.

25. Skateboard Ramp You are using wood to build
a pyramid-shaped skateboard ramp. You want each
ramp surface to incline at an angle of 30° and the
maximum height to be 56 centimeters as shown.

   a. Use the relationships shown in the diagram to
determine the lengths a, b, c, and d to the nearest
centimeter.

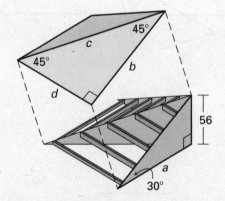

   b. Suppose you want to build a second pyramid ramp
with a 45° angle of incline and a maximum height
of 56 inches. You can use the diagram shown by
simply changing the 30° angle to 45°. Determine
the lengths a, b, c, and d to the nearest centimeter
for this ramp.

Name _____ Date _____

Find tan A and tan B. Write each answer as a decimal rounded to four decimal places.

1.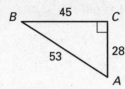

2.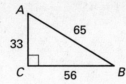

3.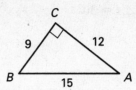

Find the value of x to the nearest tenth.

4.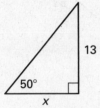

5.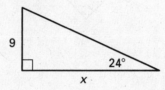

6.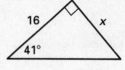

7.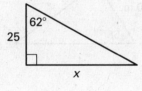

8.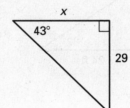

9.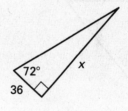

Find the value of x using the definition of tangent. Then find the value of x using the 45°-45°-90° Triangle Theorem or the 30°-60°-90° Triangle Theorem. *Compare* the results.

10.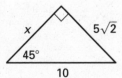

11.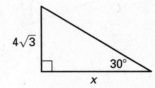

12.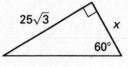

LESSON 7.5

Practice *continued*
For use with the lesson "Apply the Tangent Ratio"

**For acute ∠A of a right triangle, find tan A by using the 45°-45°-90°
Triangle Theorem or the 30°-60°-90° Triangle Theorem.**

13. $m\angle A = 30°$ **14.** $m\angle A = 45°$ **15.** $m\angle A = 60°$

Use a tangent ratio to find the value of x. Round to the nearest tenth.

16.
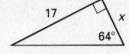

17.
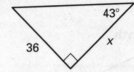

18.
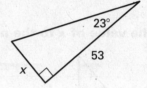

Find the area of the triangle. Round your answer to the nearest tenth.

19.
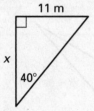

20.
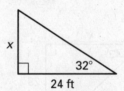

21.
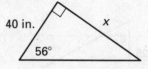

Find the perimeter of the triangle. Round to the nearest tenth.

22.
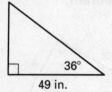

23.
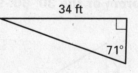

24.
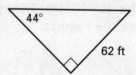

LESSON 7.5

Practice *continued*

For use with the lesson "Apply the Tangent Ratio"

25. Model Rockets To calculate the height *h* reached by a model rocket, you move 100 feet from the launch point and record the angle of elevation θ to the rocket at its highest point. The values of θ for three flights are given below. Find the rocket's height to the nearest foot for the given θ in each flight.

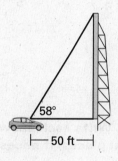

a. θ = 77°

b. θ = 81°

c. θ = 83°

26. Drive-in Movie You are 50 feet from the screen at a drive-in movie. Your eye is on a horizontal line with the bottom of the screen and the angle of elevation to the top of the screen is 58°. How tall is the screen?

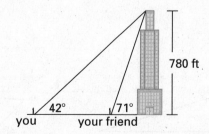

27. Skyscraper You are a block away from a skyscraper that is 780 feet tall. Your friend is between the skyscraper and yourself. The angle of elevation from your position to the top of the skyscraper is 42°. The angle of elevation from your friend's position to the top of the skyscraper is 71°. To the nearest foot, how far are you from your friend?

LESSON 7.6

Practice

For use with the lesson "Apply the Sine and Cosine Ratios"

Find sin *R* and sin *S*. Write each answer as a fraction and as a decimal. Round to four decimal places, if necessary.

1.
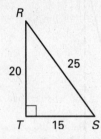

2.
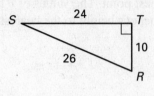

3.
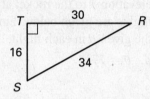

4.
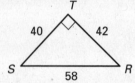

5.
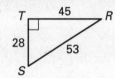

6.
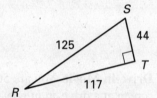

Find cos *A* and cos *B*. Write each answer as a fraction and as a decimal. Round to four decimal places, if necessary.

7.
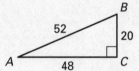

8.
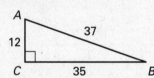

9.
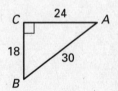

10.
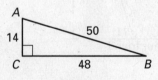

11.
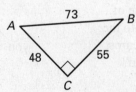

12.
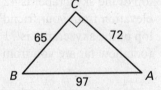

Name _____ Date _____

Practice continued
For use with the lesson "Apply the Sine and Cosine Ratios"

Use a cosine or sine ratio to find the value of each variable. Round decimals to the nearest tenth.

13.
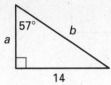

14.
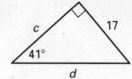

15.
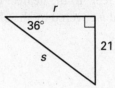

16.
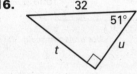

17.
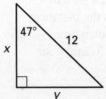

18.
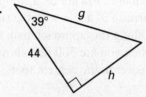

Use the 45°-45°-90° Triangle Theorem or the 30°-60°-90° Triangle Theorem to find the sine and cosine of the angle.

19. a 30° angle

20. a 45° angle

21. a 60° angle

Find the unknown side length. Then find sin *A* and cos *A*. Write each answer as a fraction in simplest form and as a decimal. Round to four decimal places, if necessary.

22.
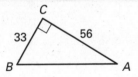

23.
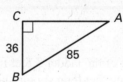

24.
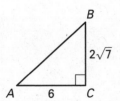

25.
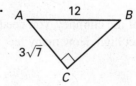

Practice continued
For use with the lesson "Apply the Sine and Cosine Ratios"

26. Ski Lift A chair lift on a ski slope has an angle of elevation of 28° and covers a total distance of 4640 feet. To the nearest foot, what is the vertical height *h* covered by the chair lift?

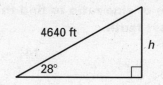

27. Airplane Landing You are preparing to land an airplane. You are on a straight line approach path that forms a 3° angle with the runway. What is the distance *d* along this approach path to your touchdown point when you are 500 feet above the ground? Round your answer to the nearest foot.

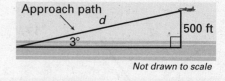

Not drawn to scale

28. Extension Ladders You are using extension ladders to paint a chimney that is 33 feet tall. The length of an extension ladder ranges in one-foot increments from its minimum length to its maximum length. For safety, you should always use an angle of about 75.5° between the ground and the ladder.

  a. Your smallest extension ladder has a maximum length of 17 feet. How high does this ladder safely reach on a vertical wall?

  b. You place the base of the ladder 3 feet from the chimney. How many feet long should the ladder be?

  c. To reach the top of the chimney, you need a ladder that reaches 30 feet high. How many feet long should the ladder be?

LESSON 7.7 Practice

For use with the lesson "Solve Right Triangles"

Use the diagram to find the indicated measurement. Round your answer to the nearest tenth.

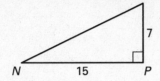

1. MN

2. $m\angle M$

3. $m\angle N$

Solve the right triangle. Round decimal answers to the nearest tenth.

4.
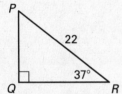

5.
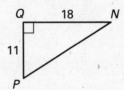

6.
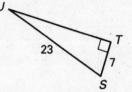

7.
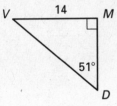

8.
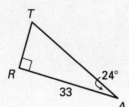

9.
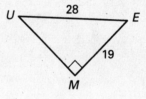

10.
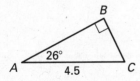

11.
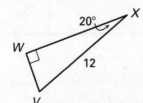

12.
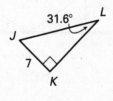

LESSON
7.7

Practice *continued*

For use with the lesson "Solve Right Triangles"

Let ∠*A* be an acute angle in a right triangle. Approximate the measure of ∠*A* to the nearest tenth of a degree.

13. $\sin A = 0.36$ **14.** $\tan A = 0.8$ **15.** $\sin A = 0.27$ **16.** $\cos A = 0.35$

17. $\tan A = 0.42$ **18.** $\cos A = 0.11$ **19.** $\sin A = 0.94$ **20.** $\cos A = 0.77$

21. Office Buildings The angle of depression from the top of a 320 foot office building to the top of a 200 foot office building is 55°. How far apart are the buildings?

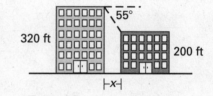

320 ft   55°   200 ft

|—*x*—|

22. Suspension Bridge Use the diagram to find the distance across the suspension bridge.

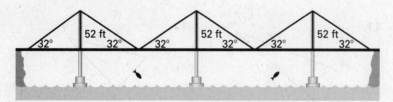

32°   52 ft   32°   32°   52 ft   32°   32°   52 ft   32°

Name _____ Date _____

In Exercises 23 and 24, use the following information.

Ramps The Uniform Federal Accessibility Standards specify that the ramp angle used for a wheelchair ramp must be less than or equal to 4.78°.

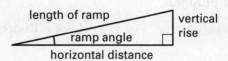

length of ramp
ramp angle
vertical rise
horizontal distance

23. The length of one ramp is 16 feet. The vertical rise is 14 inches. Estimate the ramp's horizontal distance and its ramp angle. Does this ramp meet the Uniform Federal Accessibility Standards?

24. You want to build a ramp with a vertical rise of 6 inches. You want to minimize the horizontal distance taken up by the ramp. Draw a sketch showing the approximate dimensions of your ramp.

In Exercises 25–27, use the following information.

Hot Air Balloon You are in a hot air balloon that is 600 feet above the ground where you can see two people.

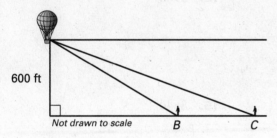

600 ft

Not drawn to scale *B* *C*

25. If the angle of depression from your line of sight to the person at *B* is 30°, how far is the person from the point on the ground below the hot air balloon?

26. If the angle of depression from your line of sight to the person at *C* is 20°, how far is the person from the point on the ground below the hot air balloon?

27. How far apart are the two people?

Name _____   Date _____

LESSON 8.1 Practice
For use with the lesson "Find Angle Measures in Polygons"

Find the sum of the measures of the interior angles of the indicated convex polygon.

1. Hexagon

2. Dodecagon

3. 11-gon

4. 15-gon

5. 20-gon

6. 40-gon

The sum of the measures of the interior angles of a convex polygon is given. Classify the polygon by the number of sides.

7. 180°

8. 540°

9. 900°

10. 1800°

11. 2520°

12. 3960°

13. 5040°

14. 5940°

15. 8640°

Find the value of x.

16.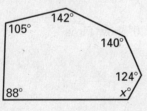

17.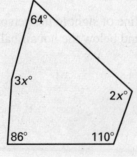

18.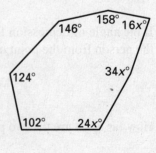

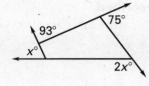

LESSON 8.1 **Practice** *continued*
For use with the lesson "Find Angle Measures in Polygons"

19.

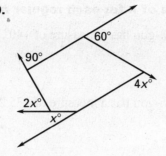

93° 75° $x°$ $2x°$

20.

60° 90° 4$x°$ 2$x°$ $x°$

21.

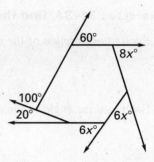

60° 8$x°$ 100° 20° 6$x°$ 6$x°$

22. What is the measure of each exterior angle of a regular nonagon?

23. The measures of the exterior angles of a convex quadrilateral are 90°, 10$x°$, 5$x°$, and 45°. What is the measure of the largest exterior angle?

24. The measures of the interior angles of a convex octagon are 45$x°$, 40$x°$, 155°, 120°, 155°, 38$x°$, 158°, and 41$x°$. What is the measure of the smallest interior angle?

Find the measures of an interior angle and an exterior angle of the indicated polygon.

25. Regular triangle

26. Regular octagon

27. Regular 16-gon

28. Regular 45-gon

29. Regular 60-gon

30. Regular 100-gon

Name _____   Date _____

In Exercises 31–34, find the value of *n* for each regular *n*-gon described.

31. Each interior angle of the regular *n*-gon has a measure of 140°.

32. Each interior angle of the regular *n*-gon has a measure of 175.2°.

33. Each exterior angle of the regular *n*-gon has a measure of 45°.

34. Each exterior angle of the regular *n*-gon has a measure of 3°.

35. Storage Shed The side view of a storage shed is shown below. Find the value of *x*. Then determine the measure of each angle.

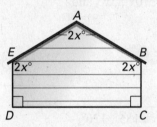

36. Tents The front view of a camping tent is shown below. Find the value of *x*. Then determine the measure of each angle.

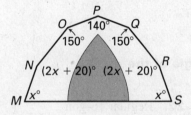

37. Proof Because all the interior angle measures of a regular *n*-gon are congruent, you can find the measure of each individual interior angle. The measure of each interior angle of a regular *n*-gon is $\frac{(n-2) \cdot 180}{n}$. Write a paragraph proof to prove this statement.

Name _____ Date _____

Find the measure of the indicated angle in the parallelogram.

1. Find $m\angle B$.

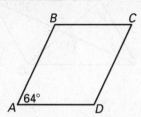

2. Find $m\angle G$.

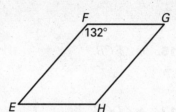

3. Find $m\angle M$.

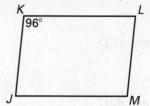

Find the value of each variable in the parallelogram.

4.

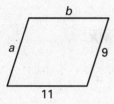

5.

6.

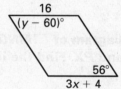

7.

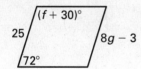

8.

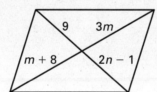

9.

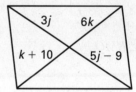

10. In $\square WXYZ$, $m\angle W$ is 50 degrees more than $m\angle X$. Sketch $\square WXYZ$. Find the measure of each interior angle. Then label each angle with its measure.

11. In $\square EFGH$, $m\angle G$ is 25 degrees less than $m\angle H$. Sketch $\square EFGH$. Find the measure of each interior angle. Then label each angle with its measure.

LESSON 8.2	**Practice** continued

For use with the lesson "Use Properties of Parallelograms"

Find the indicated measure in ☐ABCD.

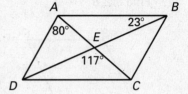

12. $m\angle AEB$

13. $m\angle BAE$

14. $m\angle AED$

15. $m\angle ECB$

16. $m\angle BAD$

17. $m\angle DCE$

18. $m\angle ADC$

19. $m\angle DCB$

Use the diagram of ☐MNOP. Points Q, R, S, and T are midpoints of $\overline{MX}$, $\overline{NX}$, $\overline{OX}$, and $\overline{PX}$. Find the indicated measure.

20. PN

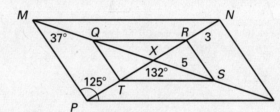

21. MQ

22. XO

23. $m\angle NMQ$

24. $m\angle NXO$

25. $m\angle MNP$

26. $m\angle NPO$

27. $m\angle NOP$

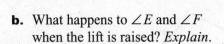

LESSON 8.2

Practice *continued*

For use with the lesson "Use Properties of Parallelograms"

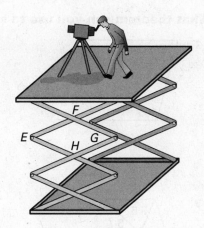

28. Movie Equipment The scissor lift shown at the right is sometimes used by camera crews to film movie scenes. The lift can be raised or lowered so that the camera can get a variety of views of one scene. In the figure, points *E*, *F*, *G*, and *H* are the vertices of a parallelogram.

   a. If $m\angle E = 45°$, find $m\angle F$.

   b. What happens to $\angle E$ and $\angle F$ when the lift is raised? *Explain.*

29. In parallelogram *RSTU*, the ratio of *RS* to *ST* is 5 : 3. Find *RS* if the perimeter of ▱*RSTU* is 64.

30. Parallelogram *MNOP* and parallelogram *PQRO* share a common side, as shown. Using a two-column proof, prove that segment *MN* is congruent to segment *QR*.

   GIVEN: *MNOP* and *PQRO* are parallelograms.

   PROVE: $\overline{MN} \cong \overline{QR}$

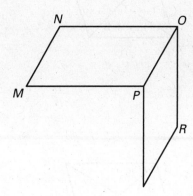

Name _____ Date _____

Practice
For use with the lesson "Show that a Quadrilateral is a Parallelogram"

What theorem can you use to show that the quadrilateral is a parallelogram?

1.
75° 105°
105°

2.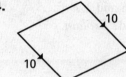
73
98   98
73

3.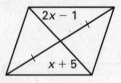
3.6
5
5
3.6

4.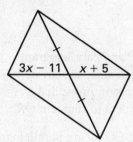
10
10

For what value of *x* is the quadrilateral a parallelogram?

5.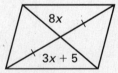
2x − 1
x + 5

6.
3x − 11   x + 5

7.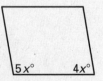
8x
3x + 5

8.
101° x°
101°

9.
5x°   4x°

10.
(5x − 7)°
(x + 1)°

LESSON 8.3 **Practice** *continued*
For use with the lesson "Show that a Quadrilateral is a Parallelogram"

The vertices of quadrilateral *ABCD* are given. Draw *ABCD* in a coordinate plane and show that it is a parallelogram.

11. $A(-2, -3), B(0, 4), C(6, 4), D(4, -3)$

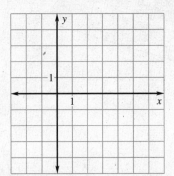

12. $A(-3, -4), B(-1, 2), C(7, 0), D(5, -6)$

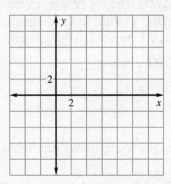

Describe how to prove that *ABCD* is a parallelogram.

13.

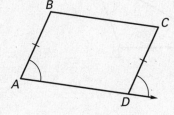

14.

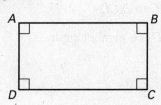

15. Three vertices of $\square ABCD$ are $A(-1, 4)$, $B(4, 4)$, and $C(11, -3)$. Find the coordinates of point D.

Practice *continued*

For use with the lesson "Show that a Quadrilateral is a Parallelogram"

16. **History** The diagram shows a battering ram which was used in ancient times to break through walls. A log is suspended on ropes of equal length ($\overline{GF}$ and $\overline{HJ}$). The log swings, causing quadrilateral *FGHJ* to shift. In the diagram, $\overline{GH} \cong \overline{FJ}$ and $\overline{GH}$ is parallel to the ground.

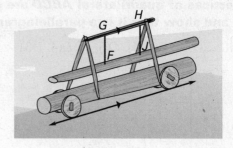

   a. Identify *FGHJ*. *Explain.*

   b. *Explain* why the log is always parallel to the ground.

17. **Proof** Use the diagram at the right.

    GIVEN: $\triangle ABC \cong \triangle CDA$

    PROVE: *ABCD* is a parallelogram.

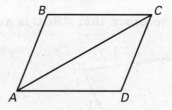

LESSON 8.4 Practice

For use with the lesson "Properties of Rhombuses, Rectangles, and Squares"

For any rhombus *ABCD*, decide whether the statement is *always* or *sometimes* true. Draw a diagram and *explain* your reasoning.

1. $\angle ABC \cong \angle CDA$

2. $\overline{CA} \cong \overline{DB}$

For any rectangle *FGHJ*, decide whether the statement is *always* or *sometimes* true. Draw a diagram and *explain* your reasoning.

3. $\angle F \cong \angle H$

4. $\overline{GH} \cong \overline{HJ}$

Classify the quadrilateral. *Explain* your reasoning.

5.

91°

6.

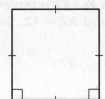

Name each quadrilateral—*parallelogram*, *rectangle*, *rhombus*, and *square*—for which the statement is true.

7. It is equilateral.

8. The diagonals are congruent.

9. It can contain obtuse angles.

10. It contains no acute angles.

LESSON 8.4 **Practice** *continued*
For use with the lesson "Properties of Rhombuses, Rectangles, and Squares"

Classify the special quadrilateral. *Explain* your reasoning. Then find the values of x and y.

11.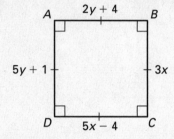

12.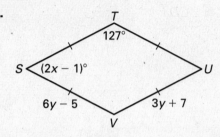

The diagonals of rhombus *PQRS* intersect at *T*.
Given that $m\angle RPS = 30°$ and $RT = 6$, find the indicated measure.

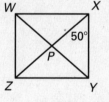

13. $m\angle QPR$ 14. $m\angle QTP$

15. RP 16. QT

The diagonals of rectangle *WXYZ* intersect at *P*.
Given that $m\angle YXZ = 50°$ and $XZ = 12$, find the indicated measure.

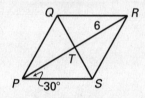

17. $m\angle WXZ$ 18. $m\angle WPX$

19. PY 20. WX

The diagonals of square *DEFG* intersect at *H*.
Given that $EH = 5$, find the indicated measure.

21. $m\angle GHF$ 22. $m\angle DGH$

23. HF 24. DE

LESSON
8.4

Practice *continued*

For use with the lesson "Properties of Rhombuses, Rectangles, and Squares"

25. Windows In preparation for a storm, a window is protected by nailing boards along its diagonals. The lengths of the boards are the same. Can you conclude that the window is square? *Explain*.

26. Clothing The side view of a wooden clothes dryer is shown at the right. Measurements shown are in inches.

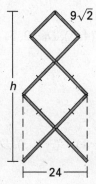

a. The uppermost quadrilateral is a square. Classify the quadrilateral below the square. *Explain* your reasoning.

b. Find the height h of the clothes dryer.

27. Proof The diagonals of rhombus *ABCD* form several triangles. Using a two-column proof, prove that $\triangle BFA \cong \triangle DFC$.

GIVEN: *ABCD* is a rhombus.

PROVE: $\triangle BFA \cong \triangle DFC$

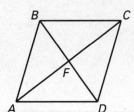

Name _____ Date _____

Points A, B, C, and D are the vertices of a quadrilateral. Determine whether ABCD is a trapezoid.

1. $A(-2, 3), B(3, 3), C(-1, -2), D(2, -2)$

2. $A(-3, 2), B(3, 0), C(4, 3), D(-2, 5)$

3. $A(-5, -3), B(-1, -1), C(-1, 3), D(-3, 2)$

Find m∠F, m∠G, and m∠H.

4.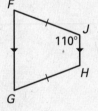

5.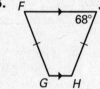

Find the length of the midsegment of the trapezoid.

6.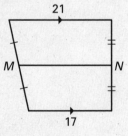

7.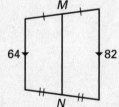

LESSON 8.5 **Practice** *continued*
For use with the lesson "Use Properties of Trapezoids and Kites"

***JKLM* is a kite. Find *m∠K*.**

8.

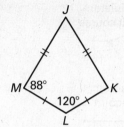

9.

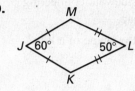

Use Theorem 8.18 and the Pythagorean Theorem to find the side lengths of the kite. Write the lengths in simplest radical form.

10.

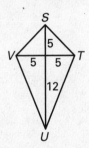

11.

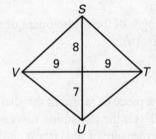

Find the value of *x*.

12.

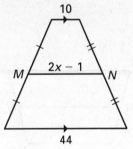

13.

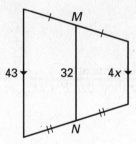

14.

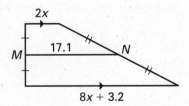

15.

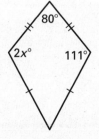

Practice continued

For use with the lesson "Use Properties of Trapezoids and Kites"

16. **Maps** Use the map shown at the right.
The lines represent a sidewalk connecting
the locations on the map.

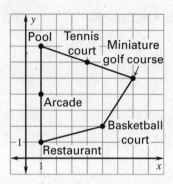

   a. Is the sidewalk in the shape of a kite?
   Explain.

   b. A sidewalk is built that connects the arcade,
   tennis court, miniature golf course, and
   restaurant. What is the shape of the
   sidewalk?

   c. What is the length of the midsegment of the
   sidewalk in part (b)?

17. **Kite** You cut out a piece of fabric in the shape of a kite so that the congruent angles
of the kite are 100°. Of the remaining two angles, one is 4 times larger than the
other. What is the measure of the largest angle in the kite?

18. **Proof** $\overline{MN}$ is the midsegment of isosceles trapezoid *FGHJ*. Write
a paragraph proof to show that *FMNJ* is an isosceles trapezoid.

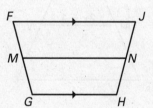

LESSON 8.6 Practice

For use with the lesson "Identify Special Quadrilaterals"

Complete the chart. Put an X in the box if the shape *always* has the given property.

	Property	▱	Rectangle	Rhombus	Square	Kite	Trapezoid
1.	Both pairs of opposite sides are congruent.						
2.	Both pairs of opposite angles are congruent.						
3.	Exactly one pair of opposite sides are congruent.						
4.	Exactly one pair of opposite sides are parallel.						
5.	Exactly one pair of opposite angles are congruent.						
6.	Consecutive angles are supplementary.						

Give the most specific name for the quadrilateral. *Explain*.

7.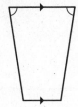

8.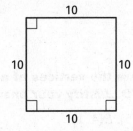

Name _____ Date _____

Practice *continued*
For use with the lesson "Identify Special Quadrilaterals"

9.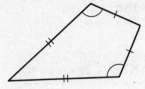

10.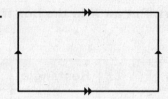

Tell whether enough information is given in the diagram to classify the quadrilateral by the indicated name.

11. Rectangle

12. Isosceles trapezoid

13. Rhombus

14. Kite

Points *A, B, C,* and *D* are the vertices of a quadrilateral. Give the most specific name for *ABCD*. *Justify* your answer.

15. $A(2, 2), B(4, 6), C(6, 5), D(4, 1)$

16. $A(-5, 1), B(0, -6), C(5, 1), D(0, 3)$

LESSON
8.6

Practice *continued*
For use with the lesson "Identify Special Quadrilaterals"

In Exercises 17 and 18, which two segments or angles must be congruent so that you can prove that *FGHJ* is the indicated quadrilateral? There may be more than one right answer.

17. Kite

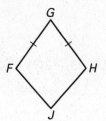

18. Isosceles trapezoid

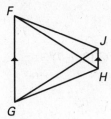

19. Picture Frame What type of special quadrilateral is the stand of the picture frame at the right?

20. Painting A painter uses a quadrilateral shaped piece of canvas. The artist begins by painting lines that represent the diagonals of the canvas. If the lengths of the painted lines are congruent, what types of quadrilaterals could represent the shape of the canvas? If the painted lines are also perpendicular, what type of quadrilateral represents the shape of the canvas?

Name _____ Date _____

Use the translation $(x, y) \rightarrow (x + 6, y - 3)$.

1. What is the image of $A(3, 2)$?

2. What is the image of $B(-4, 1)$?

3. What is the preimage of $C'(2, -7)$?

4. What is the preimage of $D'(-3, -2)$?

The vertices of $\triangle ABC$ are $A(-1, 1)$, $B(4, -1)$, and $C(2, 4)$. Graph the image of the triangle using prime notation.

5. $(x, y) \rightarrow (x - 3, y + 5)$

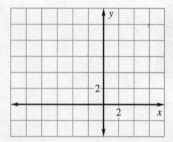

6. $(x, y) \rightarrow (x - 4, y - 2)$

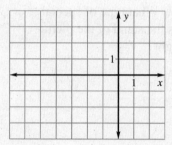

$\triangle A'B'C'$ is the image of $\triangle ABC$ after a translation. Write a rule for the translation. Then verify that the translation is an isometry.

7.

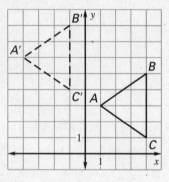

8.

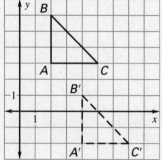

Name _____ Date _____

Name the vector and write its component form.

9.
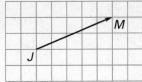

10.
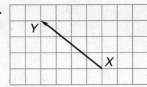

11.
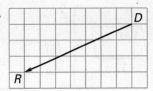

Use the point *P*(5, −2). Find the component form of the vector that describes the translation to *P*′.

12. $P'(2, 0)$ **13.** $P'(8, -3)$ **14.** $P'(0, 4)$ **15.** $P'(-5, -4)$

The vertices of △*ABC* are *A*(1, 2), *B*(2, 6), and *C*(3, 1). Translate △*ABC* using the given vector. Graph △*ABC* and its image.

16. $\langle 8, 2 \rangle$ **17.** $\langle -7, -3 \rangle$

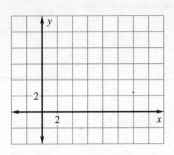   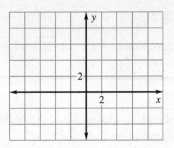

LESSON
9.1

Practice *continued*

For use with the lesson "Translate Figures and Use Vectors"

Find the value of each variable in the translation.

18.

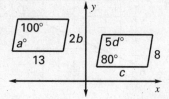

19.

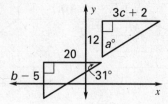

20. Navigation A hot air balloon is flying from point *A* to point *D*. After the balloon travels 6 miles east and 3 miles north, the wind direction changes at point *B*. The balloon travels to point *C* as shown in the diagram.

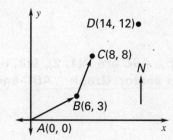

a. Write the component form for $\overrightarrow{AB}$ and $\overrightarrow{BC}$.

b. The wind direction changes and the balloon travels from point *C* to point *D*. Write the component form for $\overrightarrow{CD}$.

c. What is the total distance the balloon travels?

d. Suppose the balloon went straight from *A* to *D*. Write the component form of the vector that describes this path. What is this distance?

Practice

For use with the lesson "Use Properties of Matrices"

Use the diagram to write a matrix to represent the polygon.

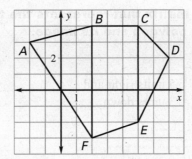

1. △*CDE*

2. △*ABF*

3. Quadrilateral *BCEF*

4. Hexagon *ABCDEF*

Add or subtract.

5. $\begin{bmatrix} 6 & 3 \end{bmatrix} + \begin{bmatrix} 1 & 9 \end{bmatrix}$

6. $\begin{bmatrix} -8 & 4 \\ 4 & -5 \end{bmatrix} + \begin{bmatrix} 4 & 6 \\ 6 & -1 \end{bmatrix}$

7. $\begin{bmatrix} 5 & -2 \\ 2 & 4 \\ -7 & 2 \end{bmatrix} + \begin{bmatrix} 1 & 3 \\ 6 & -4 \\ 6 & -1 \end{bmatrix}$

8. $\begin{bmatrix} -0.3 & 1.8 \end{bmatrix} - \begin{bmatrix} 0.6 & 2.7 \end{bmatrix}$

9. $\begin{bmatrix} -1 & -9 \\ 0 & 2 \end{bmatrix} - \begin{bmatrix} 5 & 9 \\ -6 & -7 \end{bmatrix}$

10. $\begin{bmatrix} 1.4 & 1.3 \\ -5 & -6.5 \\ 2 & 4 \end{bmatrix} - \begin{bmatrix} -1.4 & -3 \\ 3.9 & 4 \\ 1.3 & 3.9 \end{bmatrix}$

LESSON 9.2 **Practice** *continued*
For use with the lesson "Use Properties of Matrices"

Find the image matrix that represents the translation of the polygon. Then graph the polygon and its image.

11. $\begin{array}{ccc} A & B & C \end{array}$
$\begin{bmatrix} -1 & 5 & 3 \\ 2 & 2 & 6 \end{bmatrix}$; 5 units right and 3 units down

12. $\begin{array}{cccc} M & N & O & P \end{array}$
$\begin{bmatrix} 3 & 7 & 5 & 1 \\ 1 & 2 & 6 & 5 \end{bmatrix}$; 6 units left and 2 units up

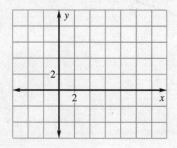

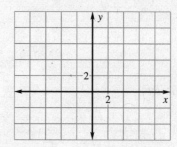

Multiply.

13. $\begin{bmatrix} 4 & -3 \end{bmatrix}\begin{bmatrix} -6 \\ 2 \end{bmatrix}$

14. $\begin{bmatrix} -0.8 & 4 \end{bmatrix}\begin{bmatrix} 3 \\ -1.6 \end{bmatrix}$

15. $\begin{bmatrix} -2 & 3 \\ 5 & -4 \end{bmatrix}\begin{bmatrix} -1 & 4 \\ 7 & 5 \end{bmatrix}$

16. $\begin{bmatrix} 0.9 & 5 \\ -4 & 2 \end{bmatrix}\begin{bmatrix} 3 & 0 \\ -4 & -3 \end{bmatrix}$

17. $\begin{bmatrix} -3 & 2 & 6 \end{bmatrix}\begin{bmatrix} -5 \\ 0 \\ -3 \end{bmatrix}$

18. $\begin{bmatrix} 2 & 5 & 5 \\ 1 & 0 & 3 \end{bmatrix}\begin{bmatrix} 0 \\ -4 \\ 2 \end{bmatrix}$

Use the described translation and the graph of the image to find the matrix that represents the preimage.

19. 3 units right and 4 units up

20. 2 units left and 3 units down

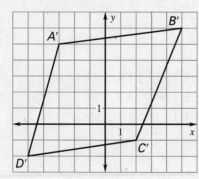

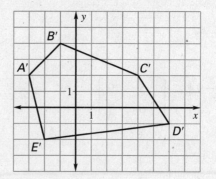

Name _____ Date _____

21. Matrix Equation Use the description of a translation of a triangle to find the value of each variable. What are the coordinates of the vertices of the image triangle?

$$\begin{bmatrix} -8 & x & -8 \\ 4 & 4 & y \end{bmatrix} + \begin{bmatrix} -2 & b & c \\ d & -5 & 2 \end{bmatrix} = \begin{bmatrix} r & -4 & -3 \\ 7 & s & 6 \end{bmatrix}$$

22. Office Supplies Two offices submit supply lists. A weekly planner costs $8, a chairmat costs $90, and a desk tray costs $5. Use matrix multiplication to find the total cost of supplies for each office.

Office 1
15 weekly planners
5 chair mats
20 desk trays

Office 2
25 weekly planners
6 chair mats
30 desk trays

23. School Play The school play was performed on three evenings. The attendance on each evening is shown in the table. Adult tickets sold for $5 and student tickets sold for $3.50.

Night	Adults	Students
First	340	250
Second	425	360
Third	440	390

a. Use matrix addition to find the total number of people that attended each night of the school play.

b. Use matrix multiplication to find how much money was collected from all tickets each night.

Practice
For use with the lesson "Perform Reflections"

Graph the reflection of the polygon in the given line.

1. *x*-axis

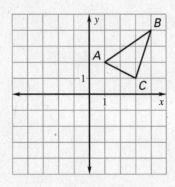

2. *y*-axis

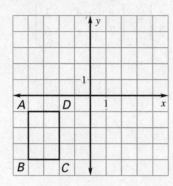

3. *x* = −1

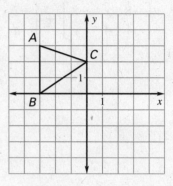

4. *y* = 1

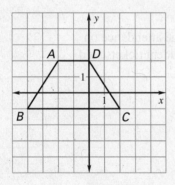

5. *y* = −*x*

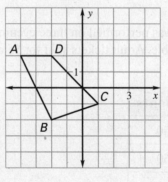

6. *y* = *x*

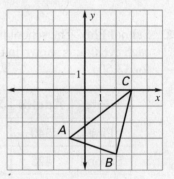

Name _____   Date _____

Use matrix multiplication to find the image. Graph the polygon and its image.

7. Reflect $\begin{bmatrix} A & B & C \\ -3 & 1 & 6 \\ 4 & 7 & 2 \end{bmatrix}$ in the x-axis.

8. Reflect $\begin{bmatrix} A & B & C & D \\ 2 & 5 & 7 & 1 \\ 6 & 4 & -5 & -3 \end{bmatrix}$ in the y-axis.

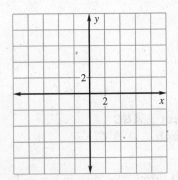

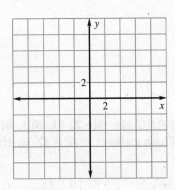

Write a matrix for the polygon. Then find the image matrix that represents the polygon after a reflection in the given line.

9. x-axis

10. y-axis

11. x-axis

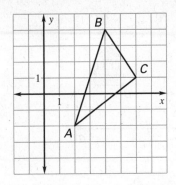

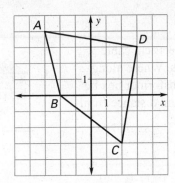

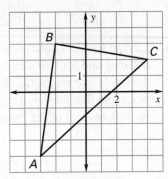

Name _____ Date _____

LESSON 9.3	**Practice** continued

For use with the lesson "Perform Reflections"

Find point _C_ on the _x_-axis so _AC_ + _BC_ is a minimum.

12. $A(2, -2), B(11, -4)$ **13.** $A(-1, 4), B(6, 3)$ **14.** $A(-3, 2), B(-6, -4)$

The vertices of △ _ABC_ are _A_(−2, 1), _B_(3, 4), and _C_(3, 1). Reflect △ _ABC_ in the first line. Then reflect △ _A′B′C′_ in the second line. Graph △ _A′B′C′_ and △ _A″B″C″_.

15. In $y = 1$, then in $y = -2$ **16.** In $x = 4$, then in $y = -1$ **17.** In $y = x$, then in $x = -2$

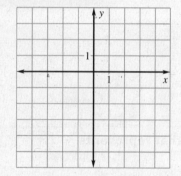   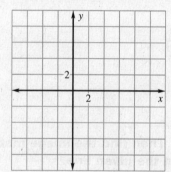   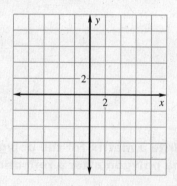

18. Laying Cable Underground electrical cable is being laid for two new homes. Where along the road (line _m_) should the transformer box be placed so that there is a minimum distance from the box to each of the homes?

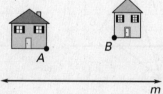

Geometry
Practice Workbook

Name _____   Date _____

LESSON 9.4 Practice

For use with the lesson "Perform Rotations"

Match the diagram with the angle of rotation.

1.

2.

3.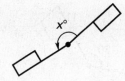

A. 110°   **B.** 170°   **C.** 50°

Trace the polygon and point *P* on paper. Then draw a rotation of the polygon the given number of degrees about *P*.

4. 45°   5. 120°   6. 135°

Rotate the figure the given number of degrees about the origin. List the coordinates of the vertices of the image.

7. 90°   8. 180°   9. 270°

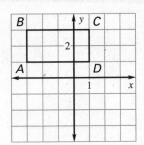   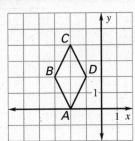   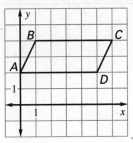

Name _____ Date _____

Find the value of each variable in the rotation.

10.

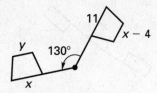

11.

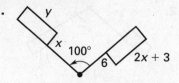

12.

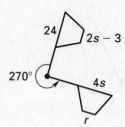

Find the image matrix that represents the rotation of the polygon about the origin. Then graph the polygon and its image.

13. $\begin{matrix} A & B & C \end{matrix}$
$\begin{bmatrix} 1 & 4 & 3 \\ 2 & 2 & 4 \end{bmatrix}; 90°$

14. $\begin{matrix} A & B & C \end{matrix}$
$\begin{bmatrix} 0 & 4 & 2 \\ -1 & 0 & 3 \end{bmatrix}; 180°$

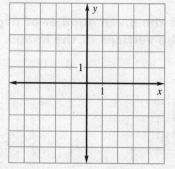

LESSON 9.4	**Practice** *continued*

For use with the lesson "Perform Rotations"

15. $\begin{bmatrix} A & B & C & D \\ 1 & 2 & 4 & 5 \\ -1 & 3 & 3 & -1 \end{bmatrix}$; 90°

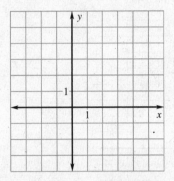

16. $\begin{bmatrix} A & B & C & D \\ -3 & -2 & 2 & 1 \\ -4 & -1 & -1 & -4 \end{bmatrix}$; 270°

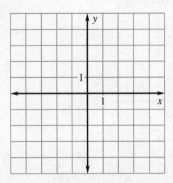

The endpoints of $\overline{CD}$ are $C(2, 1)$ and $D(4, 5)$. Graph $\overline{C'D'}$ and $\overline{C''D''}$ after the given rotations.

17. **Rotation:** 90° about the origin
   Rotation: 270° about (2, 0)

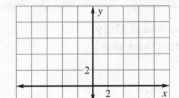

18. **Rotation:** 180° about the origin
   Rotation: 90° about (0, −3)

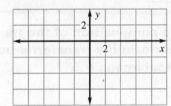

LESSON 9.5 **Practice**
For use with the lesson "Apply Compositions of Transformations"

The endpoints of $\overline{CD}$ are $C(1, 2)$ and $D(5, 4)$. Graph the image of $\overline{CD}$ after the glide reflection.

1. **Translation:** $(x, y) \rightarrow (x - 4, y)$
   Reflection: in the x-axis

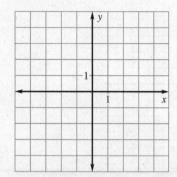

2. **Translation:** $(x, y) \rightarrow (x, y + 2)$
   Reflection: in $y = x$

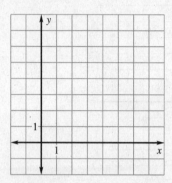

The vertices of $\triangle ABC$ are $A(3, 1)$, $B(1, 5)$, and $C(5, 3)$. Graph the image of $\triangle ABC$ after a composition of the transformations in the order they are listed.

3. **Translation:** $(x, y) \rightarrow (x + 3, y - 5)$
   Reflection: in the y-axis

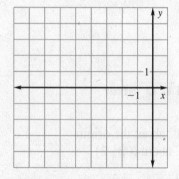

4. **Translation:** $(x, y) \rightarrow (x - 6, y + 1)$
   Rotation: 90° about the origin

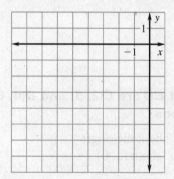

Graph $\overline{F''G''}$ after a composition of the transformations in the order they are listed. Then perform the transformations in reverse order. Does the order affect the final image $\overline{F''G''}$?

5. $F(4, -4)$, $G(1, -2)$

   Rotation: 90° about the origin
   Reflection: in the y-axis

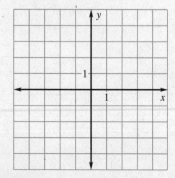

6. $F(-1, -3)$, $G(-4, -2)$

   Reflection: in the line $x = 1$
   Translation: $(x, y) \rightarrow (x + 2, y + 10)$

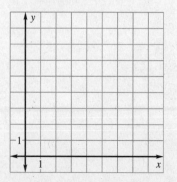

LESSON 9.5 **Practice** *continued*
For use with the lesson "Apply Compositions of Transformations"

Describe the composition of transformations.

7.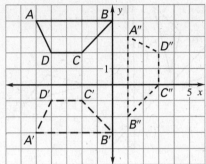

8.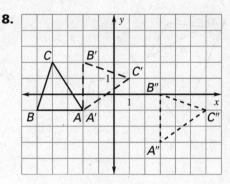

In the diagram, $k \parallel m$, $\overline{AB}$ is reflected in line k, and $\overline{A'B'}$ is reflected in line m.

9. A translation maps $\overline{AB}$ onto which segment?

10. Which lines are perpendicular to $\overleftrightarrow{BB''}$?

11. Name two segments parallel to $\overline{AA''}$.

12. If the distance between k and m is 2.7 centimeters, what is the length of $\overline{AA''}$?

13. Is the distance from A' to m the same as the distance from A'' to m? *Explain.*

**LESSON
9.5**

Practice *continued*

For use with the lesson "Apply Compositions of Transformations"

Find the angle of rotation that maps A onto A″.

14.
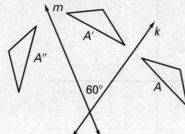

15.
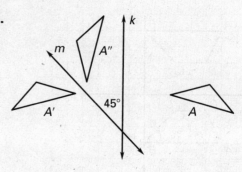

16. **Stenciling a Border** The border pattern below was made with a stencil. Describe how the border was created using one stencil four times.

Name _____ Date _____

Practice
For use with the lesson "Identify Symmetry"

Determine whether the figure has rotational symmetry. If so, describe the rotations that map the figure onto itself.

1.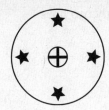

2.

3.

4.

Does the figure have the rotational symmetry shown? If not, does the figure have any rotational symmetry?

5. 120°

6. 180°

7. 45°

8. 36°

9. 180°

10. 90°

LESSON
9.6

Practice *continued*
For use with the lesson "Identify Symmetry"

In Exercises 11–16, draw a figure for the description. If not possible, write
not possible.

11. A triangle with exactly two lines of symmetry

12. A quadrilateral with exactly two lines of symmetry

13. A pentagon with exactly two lines of symmetry

14. A hexagon with exactly two lines of symmetry

15. An octagon with exactly two lines of symmetry

16. A quadrilateral with exactly four lines of symmetry

17. Paper Folding A piece of paper is folded in half and some cuts are made, as shown. Which figure represents the piece of paper unfolded?

A. **B.** **C.** 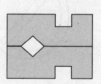 **D.**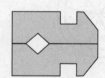

Geometry
Practice Workbook

Name _____   Date _____

LESSON 9.6 **Practice** *continued*
For use with the lesson "Identify Symmetry"

In Exercises 18 and 19, use the following information.

Taj Mahal The Taj Mahal, located in India, was built
between 1631 and 1653 by the emperor Shah Jahan as
a monument to his wife. The floor map of the Taj Mahal
is shown.

18. How many lines of symmetry does the floor
map have?

19. Does the floor map have rotational symmetry?
If so, describe a rotation that maps the pattern
onto itself.

In Exercises 20 and 21, use the following information.

Drains Refer to the diagram below of a drain in a sink.

20. Does the drain have rotational symmetry? If
so, describe the rotations that map the image
onto itself.

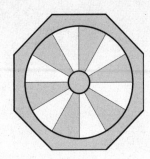

21. Would your answer to Exercise 20 change
if you disregard the shading of the figures?
Explain your reasoning.

LESSON 9.7 Practice

For use with the lesson "Identify and Perform Dilations"

Find the scale factor. Tell whether the dilation is a *reduction* or an *enlargement*. Then find the values of the variables.

1.

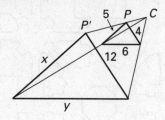

2.

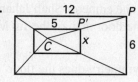

Use the origin as the center of the dilation and the given scale factor to find the coordinates of the vertices of the image of the polygon.

3. $k = 3$

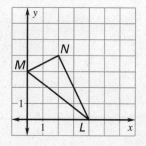

4. $k = \dfrac{1}{3}$

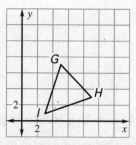

5. $k = 2$

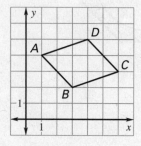

6. $k = \dfrac{5}{2}$

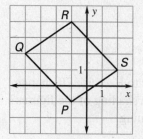

Name _____ Date _____

A dilation maps A to A' and B to B'. Find the scale factor of the dilation. Find the center of the dilation.

7. $A(4, 2), A'(5, 1), B(10, 6), B'(8, 3)$

8. $A(1, 6), A'(3, 2), B(2, 12), B'(6, 20)$

9. $A(3, 6), A'(6, 3), B(11, 10), B'(8, 4)$

10. $A(-4, 1), A'(-5, 3), B(-1, 0), B'(1, 1)$

The vertices of $\square ABCD$ are $A(1, 1), B(3, 5), C(11, 5)$, and $D(9, 1)$. Graph the image of the parallelogram after a composition of the transformations in the order they are listed.

11. **Translation:** $(x, y) \rightarrow (x + 5, y - 2)$

    Dilation: centered at the origin with a scale factor of $\frac{3}{5}$

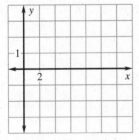

Name _____ Date _____

12. **Dilation:** centered at the origin with a scale factor of 2

Reflection: in the *x*-axis

In Exercises 13–15, use the following information.

Flashlight Image You are projecting images onto a wall with a flashlight. The lamp of the flashlight is 8.3 centimeters away from the wall. The preimage is imprinted onto a clear cap that fits over the end of the flashlight. This cap has a diameter of 3 centimeters. The preimage has a height of 2 centimeters and the lamp of the flashlight is located 2.7 centimeters from the preimage.

13. Sketch a diagram of the dilation.

14. Find the diameter of the circle of light projected onto the wall from the flashlight.

15. Find the height of the image projected onto the wall.

LESSON 10.1 Practice

For use with the lesson "Use Properties of Tangents"

Use ⊙P to draw the described part of the circle.

1. Draw a diameter and label it $\overline{AB}$.

2. Draw a tangent ray and label it $\overrightarrow{CD}$.

3. Draw a secant and label it $\overleftrightarrow{EF}$.

4. Draw a chord and label it $\overline{GH}$.

Use the diagram to determine if the statement is *true* or *false*.

5. The distance between the centers of the circles is equal to the length of the diameter of each circle.

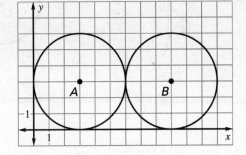

6. The lines $y = 0$ and $y = 4$ represent all the common tangents of the two circles.

7. The circles intersect at the point (6, 3).

8. Suppose the two circles shown are inscribed in a rectangle. The perimeter of the rectangle is 36 units.

LESSON	**Practice** *continued*
10.1	*For use with the lesson "Use Properties of Tangents"*

Draw two circles that have the given number of common tangents.

9. 3   **10.** 2   **11.** 0

In Exercises 12–17, $\overline{BC}$ is a radius of $\odot C$ and $\overline{AB}$ is tangent to $\odot C$. Find the value of x.

12.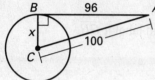

13.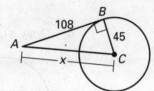

14.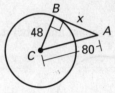

15.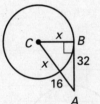

16.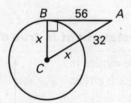

17.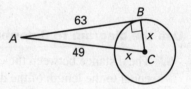

The points K and M are points of tangency. Find the value(s) of x.

18.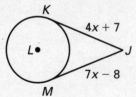

19.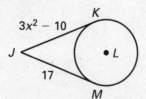

20.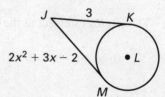

LESSON 10.1

Practice *continued*
For use with the lesson "Use Properties of Tangents"

21. Swimming Pool You are standing 36 feet from a circular swimming pool. The distance from you to a point of tangency on the pool is 48 feet as shown. What is the radius of the swimming pool?

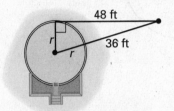

22. Space Shuttle Suppose a space shuttle is orbiting about 180 miles above Earth. What is the distance *d* from the shuttle to the horizon? The radius of Earth is about 4000 miles. Round your answer to the nearest tenth.

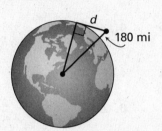

In Exercises 23 and 24, use the following information.

Golf A green on a golf course is in the shape of a circle. Your golf ball is 8 feet from the edge of the green and 32 feet from a point of tangency on the green as shown in the figure.

23. Assuming the green is flat, what is the radius of the green?

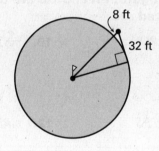

24. How far is your golf ball from the cup at the center of the green?

LESSON 10.2 Practice

For use with the lesson "Find Arc Measures"

In ⊙F, determine whether the given arc is a *minor arc*, *major arc*, or *semicircle*.

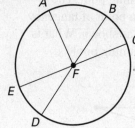

1. $\overset{\frown}{AB}$

2. $\overset{\frown}{AE}$

3. $\overset{\frown}{EAC}$

4. $\overset{\frown}{ACD}$

5. $\overset{\frown}{CAD}$

6. $\overset{\frown}{DEB}$

7. $\overset{\frown}{BAE}$

8. $\overset{\frown}{DEC}$

In the figure, $\overline{PR}$ and $\overline{QS}$ are diameters of ⊙U. Find the measure of the indicated arc.

9. $m\overset{\frown}{PQ}$

10. $m\overset{\frown}{ST}$

11. $m\overset{\frown}{TPS}$

12. $m\overset{\frown}{RT}$

13. $m\overset{\frown}{RQS}$

14. $m\overset{\frown}{QR}$

15. $m\overset{\frown}{PQS}$

16. $m\overset{\frown}{TQR}$

17. $m\overset{\frown}{PS}$

18. $m\overset{\frown}{PTR}$

**LESSON
10.2** **Practice** *continued*
For use with the lesson "Find Arc Measures"

$\overparen{PQ}$ **has a measure of 90° in ⊙R. Find the length of $\overline{PQ}$.**

19.

20.

Find the indicated arc measure.

21. $m\overparen{AC}$

22. $m\overparen{ACB}$

23. $m\overparen{DAB}$

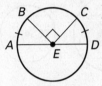

**Two diameters of ⊙T are $\overline{PQ}$ and $\overline{RS}$. Find the given arc measure
if $m\overparen{PR} = 35°$.**

24. $m\overparen{PS}$ 25. $m\overparen{PSR}$ 26. $m\overparen{PRQ}$ 27. $m\overparen{PRS}$

**Two diameters of ⊙N are $\overline{JK}$ and $\overline{LM}$. Find the given arc measure
if $m\overparen{JM} = 165°$.**

28. $m\overparen{JL}$ 29. $m\overparen{JMK}$ 30. $m\overparen{JLM}$ 31. $m\overparen{KLM}$

LESSON
10.2

Practice continued
For use with the lesson "Find Arc Measures"

Tell whether the given arcs are congruent.

32. $\overset{\frown}{JK}$ and $\overset{\frown}{QR}$

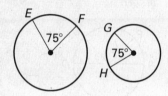

33. $\overset{\frown}{AB}$ and $\overset{\frown}{CD}$

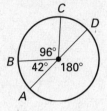

34. $\overset{\frown}{EF}$ and $\overset{\frown}{GH}$

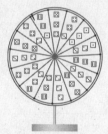

35. $\overset{\frown}{STV}$ and $\overset{\frown}{UVT}$

Game Shows **Each game show wheel shown is divided into congruent sections. Find the measure of each arc.**

36.

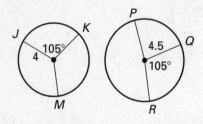

37.

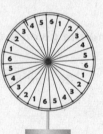

38.

In Exercises 39 and 40, use the following information.

Sprinkler A water sprinkler covers the area shown in the figure. It moves through the covered area at a rate of about 5° per second.

39. What is the measure of the arc covered by the sprinkler?

40. If the sprinkler starts at the far left position, how long will it take for the sprinkler to reach the far right position?

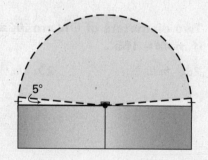

LESSON 10.3 **Practice**
For use with the lesson "Apply Properties of Chords"

Find the measure of the given arc or chord.

1. $m\overarc{BC}$

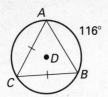

2. $m\overarc{LM}$

3. $\overline{QS}$

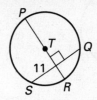

4. $m\overarc{AC}$

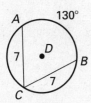

5. $m\overarc{PQR}$

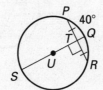

6. $m\overarc{KLM}$

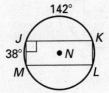

Find the value of x.

7.

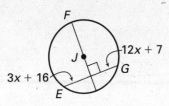

8.

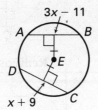

9.

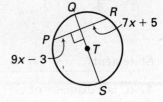

10.

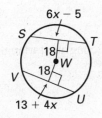

11.

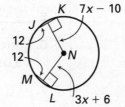

12.

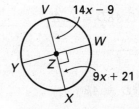

LESSON
10.3

Practice *continued*
For use with the lesson "Apply Properties of Chords"

In Exercises 13–16, determine whether $\overline{PR}$ is a diameter of the circle.

13.

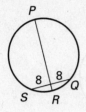

14.

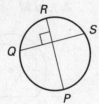

15.

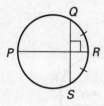

16.

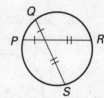

17. Proof Complete the proof.

GIVEN: $\overline{AC}$ is a diameter of $\odot F$. $\overline{AC} \perp \overline{BD}$

PROVE: $\overarc{AD} \cong \overarc{AB}$

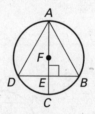

Statements	Reasons
1. $\overline{AC}$ is a diameter of $\odot F$. $\overline{AC} \perp \overline{BD}$	**1.** ?
2. ?	**2.** All right angles are congruent.
3. $\overline{DE} \cong \overline{BE}$	**3.** ?
4. $\overline{AE} \cong \overline{AE}$	**4.** ?
5. $\triangle AED \cong \triangle AEB$	**5.** ?
6. ?	**6.** Corresponding parts of congruent triangles are congruent.
7. $\overarc{AD} \cong \overarc{AB}$	**7.** ?

LESSON 10.3 **Practice** *continued*
For use with the lesson "Apply Properties of Chords"

18. Proof Complete the proof.

GIVEN: $\overline{PQ}$ is a diameter of $\odot U$. $\overset{\frown}{PT} \cong \overset{\frown}{QS}$

PROVE: $\triangle PUT \cong \triangle QUS$

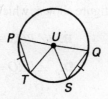

Statements	Reasons
1. $\overline{PQ}$ is a diameter of $\odot U$. $\overset{\frown}{PT} \cong \overset{\frown}{QS}$	1. __?__
2. __?__	2. Theorem 10.3
3. $\overline{UP} \cong \overline{UQ} \cong \overline{UT} \cong \overline{US}$	3. __?__
4. $\triangle PUT \cong \triangle QUS$	4. __?__

19. Briefly explain what other congruence postulate you could use to prove that $\triangle PUT \cong \triangle QUS$ in Exercise 18.

Name _____ Date _____

1. **Multiple Choice** In the figure shown, which statement is true?

   A. $\angle SPR \cong \angle PSQ$ **B.** $\angle RQS \cong \angle RPS$

   C. $\angle RPS \cong \angle PRQ$ **D.** $\angle PRQ \cong \angle SQR$

Find the measure of the indicated angle or arc in $\odot P$.

2. $m\widehat{ST}$

3. $m\widehat{AB}$

4. $m\angle JLM$

5. $m\angle A$

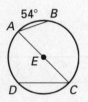

6. $m\angle K$

7. $m\widehat{VST}$

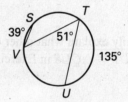

Find the measure of the indicated angle or arc in $\odot P$, given $m\widehat{LM} = 84°$ and $m\widehat{KN} = 116°$.

8. $m\angle JKL$

9. $m\angle MKL$

10. $m\angle KMN$

11. $m\angle JKM$

12. $m\angle KLN$

13. $m\angle LNM$

14. $m\widehat{MJ}$

15. $m\widehat{LKJ}$

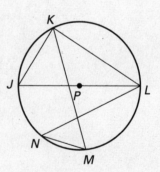

Practice *continued*
For use with the lesson "Use Inscribed Angles and Polygons"

Find the values of the variables.

16.

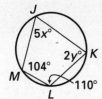

17.

18.

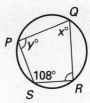

19.

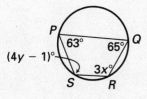

20.

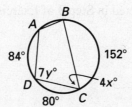

21.

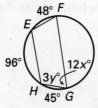

22. **Multiple Choice** What is the value of *x* in the figure shown?

A. 7   B. 12

C. 16   D. 21

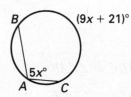

23. **Proof** Complete the proof.

GIVEN: ⊙P

PROVE: △AED ~ △BEC

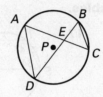

Statements	Reasons
1. ⊙P	**1.** Given
2. ?	**2.** Vertical Angles Theorem
3. ∠CAD ≅ ∠DBC	**3.** ?
4. △AED ~ △BEC	**4.** ?

24. Name two other angles that could be used in Step 3 of Exercise 23.

25. **Proof** Complete the proof.

GIVEN: $\overset{\frown}{AB}$ ≅ $\overset{\frown}{CD}$

PROVE: △ABE ≅ △DCE

Statements	Reasons
1. $\overset{\frown}{AB}$ ≅ $\overset{\frown}{CD}$	**1.** ?
2. ?	**2.** Theorem 10.3
3. ?	**3.** Vertical Angles Theorem
4. ∠BDC ≅ ∠CAB	**4.** ?
5. △ABE ≅ △DCE	**5.** ?

LESSON 10.5

Practice
For use with the lesson "Apply Other Angle Relationships in Circles"

Find the indicated arc measure.

1. $m\widehat{AB}$

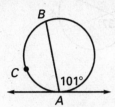

2. $m\widehat{FH}$

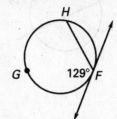

3. $m\widehat{JKL}$

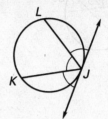

Find $m\angle 1$.

4.

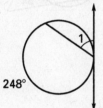

5.

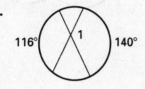

6.

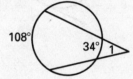

7.

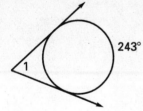

8.

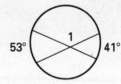

9.

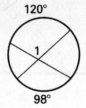

10.

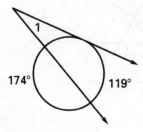

11.

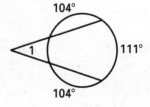

12.

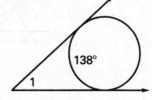

Practice *continued*
For use with the lesson "Apply Other Angle Relationships in Circles"

In Exercises 13–18, find the value of *x*.

13.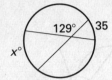

14.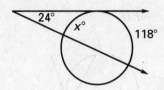

15.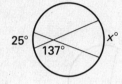

16.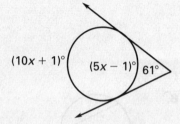

17.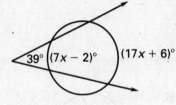

18.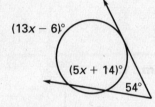

19. In the diagram shown, *m* is tangent to the circle at the point *S*. Find the measures of all the numbered angles.

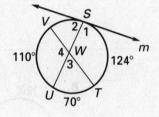

Use the diagram shown to find the measure of the angle.

20. *m∠CAF*

21. *m∠AFB*

22. *m∠CEF*

23. *m∠CFB*

24. *m∠DCF*

25. *m∠BCD*

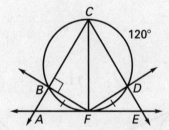

LESSON 10.5

Practice *continued*

For use with the lesson "Apply Other Angle Relationships in Circles"

In Exercises 26 and 27, the circles are concentric. Find the value of x.

26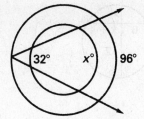

27.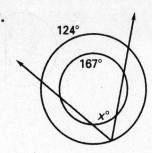

28. **Transportation** A plane is flying at an altitude of about 7 miles above Earth. What is the measure of arc *TV* that represents the part of Earth you can see? The radius of Earth is about 4000 miles.

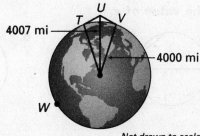

Not drawn to scale

29. **Mountain Climbing** A mountain climber is standing on top of a mountain that is about 4.75 miles above sea level. Use the information from Exercise 28 to find the measure of the arc that represents the part of Earth the mountain climber can see.

Name _____ Date _____

Find the value of x.

1.

23
23   15
x

2.

3
6   x
4

3.

x
6   x + 4
12

Find AB and DE.

4.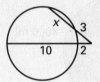

E
12
x + 5   6
A   B
D   x

5.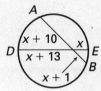

A
x + 10   x
D   x + 13   E
B
x + 1

6.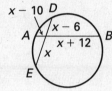

x − 10   D
x − 6
A   x + 12   B
x
E

Find the value of x.

7.

x   3
10   2

8.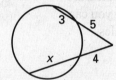

3   5
x   4

9.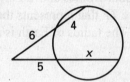

4
6
x
5

Find RT and TV.

10.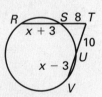

R   S 8 T
x + 3
10
x − 3   U
V

11.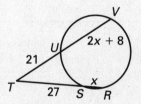

V
2x + 8
U
21
x
T
27   S   R

12.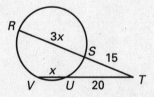

R
3x
S   15
x
V   U   20   T

Find the value of x.

13.

10
5
x

14.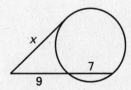

x
7
9

15.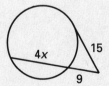

15
4x
9

LESSON 10.6 **Practice** *continued*
For use with the lesson *"Find Segment Lengths in Circles"*

Find *PQ*.

16.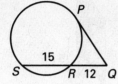

17.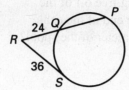

18.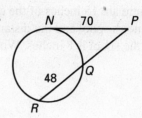

Find the value of *x*.

19.

20.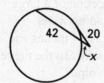

21.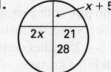

22.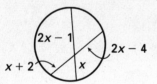

23.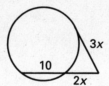

24.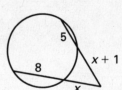

25.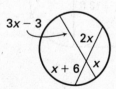

26.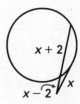

27.

LESSON
10.6
Practice *continued*
For use with the lesson "Find Segment Lengths in Circles"

28. Winch A large industrial winch is enclosed as shown.
There are 15 inches of the cable hanging free off of the
winch's spool and the distance from the end of the cable
to the spool is 8 inches. What is the diameter of the spool?

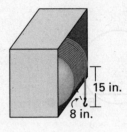

15 in.

8 in.

29. Storm Drain The diagram shows a cross-section of a large
storm drain pipe with a small amount of standing water.
The distance across the surface of the water is 48 inches and
the water is 4.25 inches deep at its deepest point. To the nearest
inch, what is the diameter of the storm drain pipe?

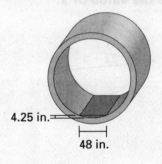

4.25 in.

48 in.

30. Basketball The Xs show the positions of two basketball
teammates relative to the circular "key" on a basketball
court. The player outside the key passes the ball to the
player on the key. To the nearest tenth of a foot, how
long is the pass?

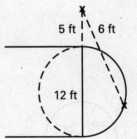

5 ft   6 ft

12 ft

LESSON
10.7

Practice

For use with the lesson "Write and Graph Equations of Circles"

Write the standard equation of the circle.

1.

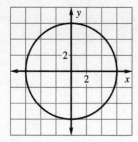

2.

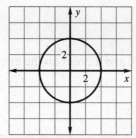

3.

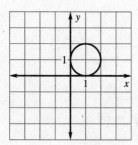

4.

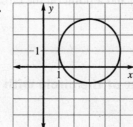

Write the standard equation of the circle with the given center and radius.

5. Center $(0, 0)$, radius 9

6. Center $(1, 3)$, radius 4

7. Center $(-3, 0)$, radius 5

8. Center $(4, -7)$, radius 13

9. Center $(0, 14)$, radius 14

10. Center $(-12, 7)$, radius 6

Use the given information to write the standard equation of the circle.

11. The center is $(0, 0)$, and a point on the circle is $(4, 0)$.

12. The center is $(0, 0)$, and a point on the circle is $(3, -4)$.

Practice *continued*
For use with the lesson *"Write and Graph Equations of Circles"*

13. The center is $(2, 4)$, and a point on the circle is $(-3, 16)$.

14. The center is $(3, -2)$, and a point on the circle is $(23, 19)$.

15. The center is $(-43, 5)$, and a point on the circle is $(-34, 17)$.

16. The center is $(17, 24)$, and a point on the circle is $(-3, 9)$.

Determine the diameter of the circle with the given equation.

17. $x^2 + y^2 = 100$

18. $(x - 12)^2 + (y + 5)^2 = 64$

19. $(x - 2)^2 + (y - 9)^2 = 4$

20. $(x + 16)^2 + (y + 15)^2 = 81$

Graph the equation.

21. $x^2 + y^2 = 64$

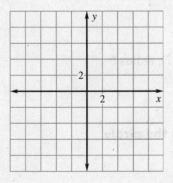

22. $(x - 4)^2 + (y + 1)^2 = 16$

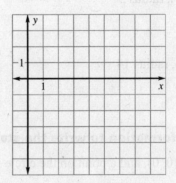

Date _____

Determine whether the point lies on the circle described by the equation
$(x - 3)^2 + (y - 8)^2 = 100$.

23. $(0, 0)$ **24.** $(13, 8)$ **25.** $(-5, 2)$ **26.** $(11, 5)$

27. Earthquakes After an earthquake, you are given seismograph readings from three locations, where the coordinate units are miles.

At $A(2, 1)$, the epicenter is 5 miles away.

At $B(-2, -2)$, the epicenter is 6 miles away.

At $C(-6, 4)$, the epicenter is 4 miles away.

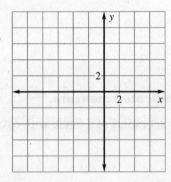

a. Graph three circles in one coordinate plane to represent the possible epicenter locations determined by each of the seismograph readings.

b. What are the coordinates of the epicenter?

c. People could feel the earthquake up to 9 miles from its epicenter. Could a person at $(4, -5)$ feel it? *Explain.*

28. Olympic Flag You are using a math software program to design a pattern for an Olympic flag. In addition to the dimensions shown in the diagram, the distance between any two adjacent rings in the same row is 3 inches.

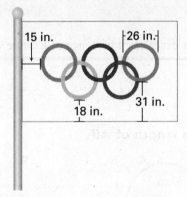

a. Use the given dimensions to write equations representing the outer circles of the five rings. Use inches as units in a coordinate plane with the lower left corner of the flag at the origin.

b. Each ring is 3 inches thick. *Explain* how you can adjust the equations of the outer circles to write equations representing the inner circles.

Name _____ Date _____

Use the diagram to find the indicated measure.

1. Find the circumference.

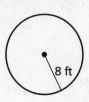

8 ft

2. Find the circumference.

13 in.

3. Find the radius.

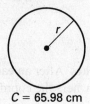

r

$C = 65.98$ cm

Find the indicated measure.

4. The exact radius of a circle with circumference 42 meters

5. The exact diameter of a circle with circumference 39 centimeters

6. The exact circumference of a circle with diameter 15 inches

7. The exact circumference of a circle with radius 27 feet

Find the length of $\widehat{AB}$.

8.

6 cm
60°
P   B

9.

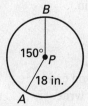

B
150°
P
18 in.
A

10.

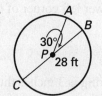

A
B
30°
P
28 ft
C

Name _____ Date _____

In ⊙D shown below, ∠EDF ≅ ∠FDG. Find the indicated measure.

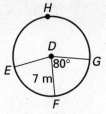

11. $m\widehat{EFG}$ **12.** $m\widehat{EHG}$ **13.** Length of $\widehat{EFG}$

14. Length of $\widehat{EHG}$ **15.** $m\widehat{EHF}$ **16.** Length of $\widehat{FEG}$

Find the indicated measure.

17. $m\widehat{AB}$ **18.** Circumference of ⊙F   **19.** Radius of ⊙J

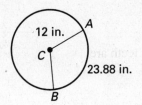   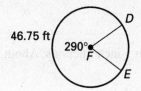   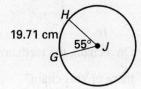

Find the perimeter of the region.

20.

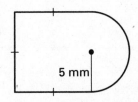

21.

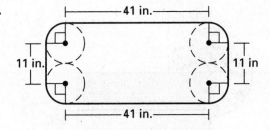

Practice continued
For use with the lesson "Circumference and Arc Length"

22. In the table below, $\overset{\frown}{AB}$ refers to the arc of a circle. Complete the table.

Radius	4	11			9.5	10.7
$m\overset{\frown}{AB}$	30°		105°	75°		270°
Length of $\overset{\frown}{AB}$		8.26	17.94	6.3	14.63	

23. Bicycles The chain of a bicycle travels along the front and rear sprockets, as shown. The circumference of each sprocket is given.

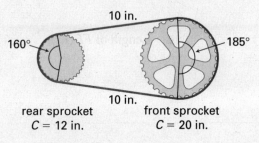

10 in.

160°   185°

10 in.

rear sprocket   front sprocket
C = 12 in.   C = 20 in.

a. About how long is the chain?

b. On a chain, the teeth are spaced in $\frac{1}{2}$ inch intervals. About how many teeth are there on this chain?

24. Enclosing a Garden You have planted a circular garden adjacent to one of the corners of your garage, as shown. You want to fence in your garden. About how much fencing do you need?

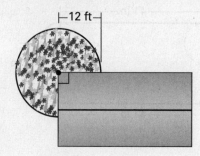

├—12 ft—┤

LESSON 11.2 **Practice**
For use with the lesson "Areas of Circles and Sectors"

Find the exact area of the circle. Then find the area to the nearest hundredth.

1.
6 in.

2.
10.5 ft

3.
24.8 cm

Find the indicated measure.

4. The area of a circle is 173 square inches. Find the radius.

5. The area of a circle is 290 square meters. Find the radius.

6. The area of a circle is 654 square centimeters. Find the diameter.

7. The area of a circle is 528 square feet. Find the diameter.

Find the areas of the sectors formed by ∠ACB.

8.
4 in.
65°

9.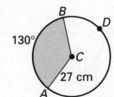
130°
27 cm

10.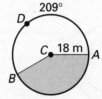
209°
18 m

Practice *continued*
For use with the lesson "Areas of Circles and Sectors"

Use the diagram to find the indicated measure.

11. Find the area of ⊙H. **12.** Find the radius of ⊙H. **13.** Find the diameter of ⊙H.

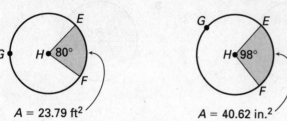

A = 23.79 ft²   *A* = 40.62 in.²   *A* = 31.47 m²

**The area of ⊙R is 295.52 square inches. The area of sector PRQ is
55 square inches. Find the indicated measure.**

14. Radius of ⊙R   **15.** Circumference of ⊙R

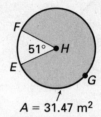

16. m⌢PQ   **17.** Length of ⌢PQ

18. Perimeter of shaded region **19.** Perimeter of unshaded region

Find the area of the shaded region.

20.   **21.**   **22.**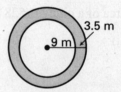

23. 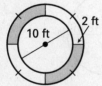   **24.** 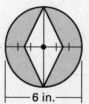   **25.**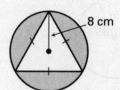

Name _____ Date _____

Practice *continued*
For use with the lesson "Areas of Circles and Sectors"

26. Fountain A circular water fountain has a diameter of 42 feet. Find the area of the fountain.

27. Landscaping The diagram at the right shows the area of a lawn covered by a water sprinkler.

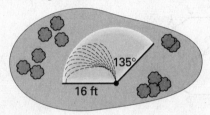

135°

16 ft

a. What is the area of the lawn that is covered by the sprinkler?

b. The water pressure is weakened so that the radius is 10 feet. What is the area of lawn that will be covered?

28. Window Design The window shown is in the shape of a semicircle. Find the area of the glass in the shaded region.

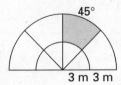

45°

3 m 3 m

Name _____   Date _____

Practice
For use with the lesson "Areas of Regular Polygons"

Find the measure of a central angle of a regular polygon with the given number of sides. Round answers to the nearest tenth of a degree, if necessary.

1. 20 sides

2. 36 sides

3. 120 sides

4. 23 sides

Find the given angle measure for the regular dodecagon shown.

5. $m\angle TWU$

6. $m\angle TWX$

7. $m\angle XUW$

8. $m\angle TWK$

9. $m\angle UWK$

10. $m\angle XWK$

11. Multiple Choice Which expression gives the apothem for a regular nonagon with side length 10.5?

A. $a = \dfrac{5.25}{\tan 40°}$

B. $a = \dfrac{10.5}{\tan 20°}$

C. $a = \dfrac{5.25}{\tan 20°}$

D. $a = 5.25 \cdot \tan 20°$

12. A regular hexagon has diameter 22 inches. What is the length of its apothem? Round your answer to the nearest tenth.

13. A regular octagon has diameter 8.5 feet. What is the length of its apothem? Round your answer to the nearest tenth.

Name _____   Date _____

Find the perimeter and area of the regular polygon. Round answers to the nearest tenth, if necessary.

14.

15.

20

16.

5

17.

4.5

18.

5

19.

2.5

20. What is the area of a regular 18-gon with a side length of 8 meters? Round your answer to the nearest tenth, if necessary.

21. What is the area of a regular 24-gon with a side length of 10 inches? Round your answer to the nearest tenth, if necessary.

22. What is the area of a regular 30-gon with a radius of 20 feet? Round your answer to the nearest tenth, if necessary.

23. Find the area of a regular pentagon inscribed in a circle whose equation is given by $(x - 4)^2 + (y - 6)^2 = 16$.

24. Find the area of a regular octagon inscribed in a circle whose equation is given by $(x - 2)^2 + (y + 3)^2 = 25$.

Practice *continued*
For use with the lesson "Areas of Regular Polygons"

Find the area of the shaded region. Round answers to the nearest tenth, if necessary.

25.

26.

27.

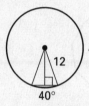

28.

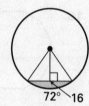

In Exercises 29 and 30, use the following information.

Tiles You are tiling the floor of a hallway with tiles that are regular hexagons as shown.

29. What is the area of each tile?

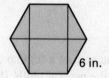

6 in.

30. The hallway has a width of 5 feet and a length of 12 feet. At least how many tiles will you need?

31. A cup saucer is shaped like a regular decagon with a diameter of 5.5 inches as shown.

   a. What is the length of the apothem of the saucer? Round your answer to the nearest tenth.

   b. What is the perimeter and area of the saucer? Round your answers to the nearest tenth.

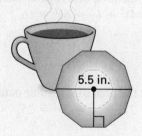

5.5 in.

LESSON 11.4 Practice

For use with the lesson "Use Geometric Probability"

Find the probability that a point *K*, selected randomly on $\overline{AE}$, is on the given segment. Express your answer as a fraction, decimal, and percent.

A   B   C   D   E
-8 -6 -4 -2 0   2   4   6   8

1. $\overline{BC}$ **2.** $\overline{BD}$ **3.** $\overline{CE}$ **4.** $\overline{AD}$

Find the probability that a randomly chosen point in the figure lies in the shaded region.

5.

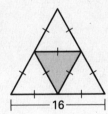

6
8

6.

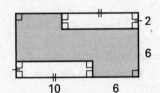

2
6
10   6

7.

6

8.

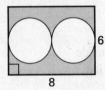

16

9.

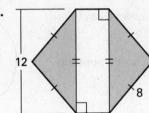

12
8
4

10.

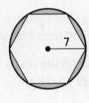

7

Find the probability that a point chosen at random on the segment satisfies the inequality.

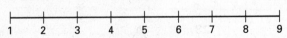

1   2   3   4   5   6   7   8   9

11. $x + 3 \le 5$ **12.** $2x - 3 \le 3$ **13.** $3x + 5 \ge 17$ **14.** $2x - 12 \ge 8$

LESSON
11.4 **Practice** continued
For use with the lesson "Use Geometric Probability"

Use the scale drawing.

15. What is the approximate area of the shaded figure in the scale drawing?

16. Find the probability that a randomly chosen point lies in the shaded region.

17. Find the probability that a randomly chosen point lies outside of the shaded region.

18. **Boxes and Buckets** A circular bucket with a diameter of 18 inches is placed inside a two foot cubic box. A small ball is thrown into the box. Find the probability that the ball lands in the bucket.

In Exercises 19 and 20, use the following information.

Arcs and Sectors The figure to the right shows a circle with a sector that intercepts an arc of 60°.

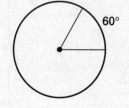

19. Find the probability that a randomly chosen point on the circle lies on the arc.

20. Find the probability that a randomly chosen point in the circle lies in the sector.

Find the probability that a randomly chosen point in the figure lies in the shaded region.

21.

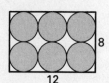

12

8

22.

4   4
2

23.

6

1.5

Name _____ Date _____

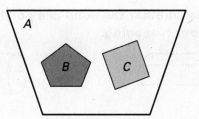

24. Multiple Choice A point X is chosen at random in region A, and A includes region B and region C. What is the probability that X is not in B?

A. $\dfrac{\text{Area of } A + \text{Area of } C}{\text{Area of } A}$

B. $\dfrac{\text{Area of } A + \text{Area of } C - \text{Area of } B}{\text{Area of } A + \text{Area of } C}$

C. $\dfrac{\text{Area of } A - \text{Area of } B}{\text{Area of } A}$

25. Subway At the local subway station, a subway train is scheduled to arrive every 15 minutes. The train waits for 2 minutes while passengers get off and on, and then departs for the next station. What is the probability that there is a train waiting when a pedestrian arrives at the station at a random time?

In Exercises 26–28, use the following information.

School Day The school day consists of six block classes with each being 60 minutes long. Lunch is 25 minutes. Transfer time between classes and/or lunch is 3 minutes. There is a fire drill scheduled to happen at a random time during the day.

26. What is the probability that the fire drill begins during lunch?

27. What is the probability that the fire drill begins during transfer time?

28. If you are 2 hours late to school, what is the probability that you missed the fire drill?

Name _____ Date _____

Practice

For use with the lesson "Explore Solids"

Determine whether the solid is a polyhedron. If it is, name the polyhedron. *Explain* your reasoning.

1.

2.

3.

Use Euler's Theorem to find the value of *n*.

4. Faces: *n*
   Vertices: 4
   Edges: 6

5. Faces: 10
   Vertices: *n*
   Edges: 24

6. Faces: 14
   Vertices: 24
   Edges: *n*

Sketch the polyhedron.

7. Triangular pyramid

8. Pentagonal pyramid

9. Hexagonal prism

Name _____ Date _____

LESSON
11.5

Practice *continued*
For use with the lesson "Explore Solids"

**Find the number of faces, vertices, and edges of the polyhedron.
Check your answer using Euler's Theorem.**

10.
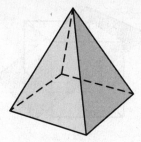

11.
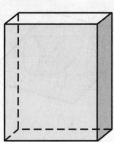

12.
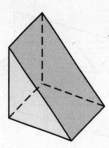

13.
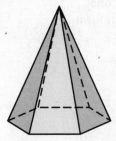

14.
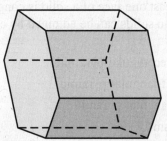

15.
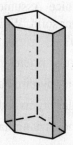

16. Visual Thinking An architect is designing a contemporary office building in the shape of a pyramid. The building will have eight sides. What is the shape of the base of the building?

Determine whether the solid is *convex* or *concave*.

17.
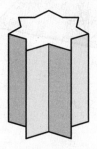

18.
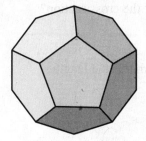

19.
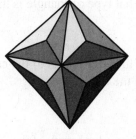

Practice *continued*
For use with the lesson "Explore Solids"

Describe the cross section formed by the intersection of the plane and the solid.

20.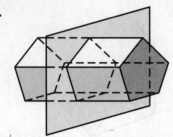

21.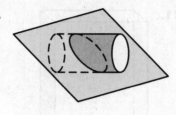

22.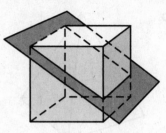

23. Multiple Choice Assume at least one face of a solid is congruent to at least one face of another solid. Which two solids can be adjoined by congruent faces to form a hexahedron?

A. A rectangular prism and a rectangular pyramid

B. A triangular pyramid and a triangular pyramid

C. A triangular prism and a triangular pyramid

D. A cube and a triangular prism

24. Reasoning Of the four possible solid combinations in Exercise 23, which combination has the most faces? How many faces are there?

In Exercises 25–27, use the following information.

Cross Section The figure at the right shows a cube that is intersected by a diagonal plane. The cross section passes through three vertices of the cube.

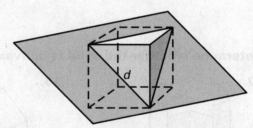

25. What type of triangle is the shape of the cross section?

26. If the edge length of the cube is 1, what is the length of the line segment d?

27. If the edge length of the cube is $4\sqrt{2}$, what is the perimeter of the cross section?

Name _____   Date _____

Practice

For use with the lesson "Volume of Prisms and Cylinders"

Find the volume of the solid by determining how many unit cubes are contained in the solid.

1.

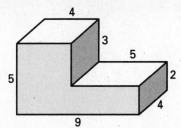

2.

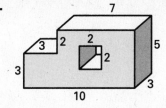

3.

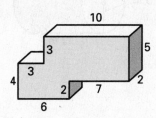

Find the volume of the right prism or right cylinder. Round your answer to two decimal places.

4.

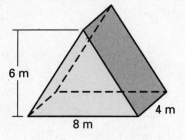

5.

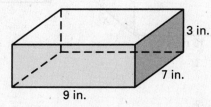

6.

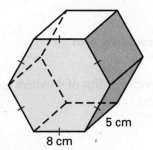

7.

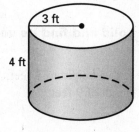

Practice *continued*
For use with the lesson "Volume of Prisms and Cylinders"

8.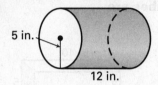

9.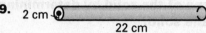

Find the length *x* using the given volume *V*.

10. $V = 1440 \text{ m}^3$

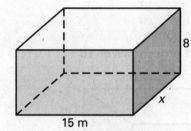

11. $V = 360 \text{ ft}^3$

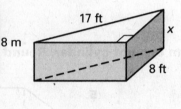

12. $V = 72\pi \text{ cm}^3$

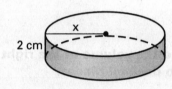

13. **Multiple Choice** How many 2 inch cubes can fit completely in a box that is 10 inches long, 8 inches wide, and 4 inches tall?

   A. 24   **B.** 32   **C.** 40   **D.** 320

Sketch the described solid and find its volume. Round your answer to two decimal places.

14. A rectangular prism with a height of 3 feet, width of 6 feet, and length of 9 feet.

15. A right cylinder with a radius of 4 meters and a height of 8 meters.

LESSON 11.6 **Practice** *continued*
For use with the lesson *"Volume of Prisms and Cylinders"*

Find the volume of the solid. The prisms and cylinders are right. Round your answer to two decimal places.

16.

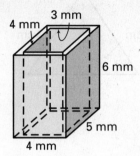

4 mm 3 mm
6 mm
5 mm
4 mm

17.

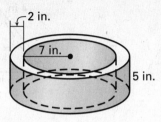

2 in.
7 in.
5 in.

Use Cavalieri's Principle to find the volume of the oblique prism or cylinder. Round your answer to two decimal places.

18.

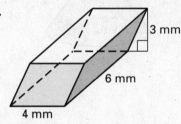

3 mm
6 mm
4 mm

19.

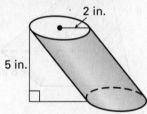

2 in.
5 in.

20.

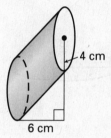

4 cm
6 cm

In Exercises 21–23, use the following information.

Pillars In order to model a home, you need to create four miniature pillars out of plaster of paris. The pillars will be shaped as regular hexagonal prisms with a face width of 2 inches and a height of 12 inches. Round your answers to two decimal places.

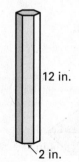

12 in.

2 in.

21. What is the area of the base of a pillar?

22. How much plaster of paris is needed for one pillar?

23. Is 480 cubic inches enough plaster of paris for all four pillars?

LESSON
11.7

Practice

For use with the lesson "Volume of Pyramids and Cones"

Find the volume of the solid. Round your answer to two decimal places.

1.

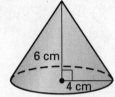

6 cm
4 cm

2.

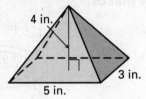

4 in.
3 in.
5 in.

3.

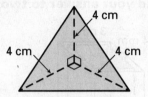

4 cm
4 cm
4 cm
4 cm

4.

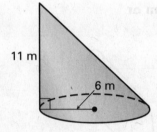

11 m
6 m

5.

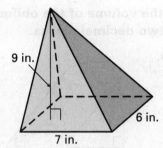

9 in.
6 in.
7 in.

6.

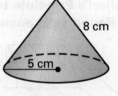

8 cm
5 cm

Find the value of *x*.

7. $V = 64$ in.^{3}

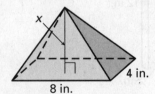

x
8 in.
4 in.

8. $V = 147\pi$ cm^3

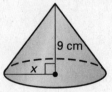

9 cm
x

9. $V = 56$ m^3

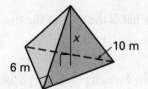

x
6 m
10 m

LESSON
11.7

Practice *continued*
For use with the lesson "Volume of Pyramids and Cones"

10. **Multiple Choice** A right cone has a height of 6 feet and a volume of 32π cubic feet. What is its radius?

    A. 2 ft   **B.** 3 ft

    C. 4 ft   **D.** 5 ft

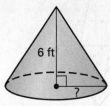

Find the volume of the right cone. Round your answer to two decimal places.

11.

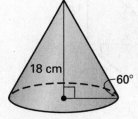

12.

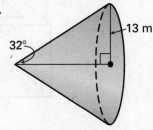

13.

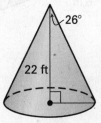

Find the volume of the solid. The prisms, pyramids, and cones are right. Round your answer to two decimal places.

14.

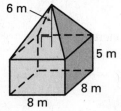

15.

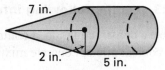

Name _____ Date _____

16.

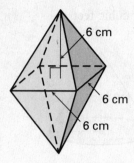

6 cm
6 cm
6 cm

17.

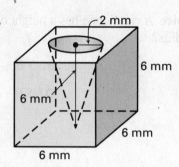

2 mm
6 mm
6 mm
6 mm
6 mm

18.

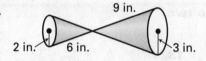

9 in.
2 in. 6 in. 3 in.

19.

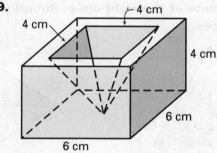

4 cm
4 cm
4 cm
6 cm
6 cm

20. Height of a Pyramid A right pyramid with a square base has a volume of 16 cubic feet. The height is six times the base edge length. What is the height of the pyramid?

In Exercises 21–23, use the following information.

Concrete To complete a construction job, a contractor needs 78 cubic yards of concrete. The contractor has a conical pile of concrete mix that measures 22 feet in diameter and 12 feet high.

21. How many cubic feet of concrete are available to the contractor?

22. How many cubic yards of concrete are available to the contractor?

23. Does the contractor have enough concrete to finish the job?

Name _____   Date _____

LESSON 11.8 **Practice**
For use with the lesson "Surface Area and Volume of Spheres"

Find the surface area of the sphere. Round your answer to two decimal places.

1.
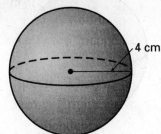
4 cm

2.
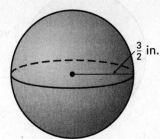
$\frac{3}{2}$ in.

3.
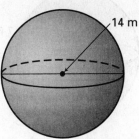
14 m

4. **Multiple Choice** What is the approximate radius of a sphere with a surface area of 40π square feet?

   A. 2 ft   **B.** 3.16 ft   **C.** 6.32 ft   **D.** 10 ft

In Exercises 5–7, use the sphere below. The center of the sphere is *C* and its circumference is 7π centimeters.

5. Find the radius of the sphere.

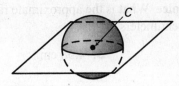

6. Find the diameter of the sphere.

7. Find the surface area of one hemisphere.
   Round your answer to two decimal places.

8. **Great Circle** The circumference of a great circle of a sphere is 24.6π meters. What is the surface area of the sphere? Round your answer to two decimal places.

Practice *continued*
For use with the lesson "Surface Area and Volume of Spheres"

Find the volume of the sphere. Round your answer to two decimal places.

9. 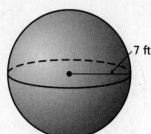 7 ft

10. 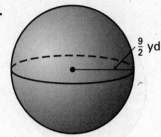 $\frac{9}{2}$ yd

11. 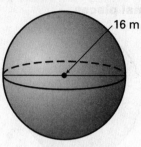 16 m

Find the radius of the sphere with the given volume *V*. Round your answer to two decimal places.

12. $V = 64$ in.^{3}

13. $V = 150\pi$ cm^3

14. $V = 152$ m^3

15. **Multiple Choice** What is the approximate radius of a sphere with a volume of 128π cubic centimeters?

   A. 2.5 cm   **B.** 4.58 cm   **C.** 6.62 cm   **D.** 8 cm

Find the surface area and the volume of the solid. The cylinders and cones are right. Round your answer to two decimal places.

16. 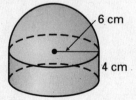 6 cm   4 cm

17. 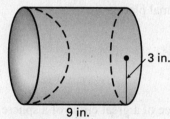 3 in.   9 in.

18. 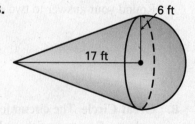 6 ft   17 ft

Name _____   Date _____

Complete the table below. Leave your answers in terms of π.

	Radius of sphere	Circumference of great circle	Surface area of sphere	Volume of sphere
19.	12 mm			
20.		8π in.		
21.			49π ft^2	
22.				288π m^3

23. **Finding a Diameter** The volume of a sphere is 972π cubic centimeters. What is the diameter of the sphere?

In Exercises 24–26, use the following information.

Golf Balls A standard golf ball has a diameter of 1.68 inches. Golf balls are often sold in a box of four. Assume that the balls are packed tightly so that they touch the lateral sides and the bases of the box.

24. What is the surface area of a golf ball?

25. What is the volume of a golf ball?

26. What is the amount of volume inside the box that is not taken up by the golf balls?

Name _____ Date _____

Tell whether the pair of right solids is similar. If so, determine the scale factor.

1.
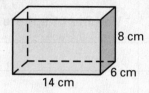
8 cm
6 cm
14 cm
4 cm
3 cm
7 cm

2.
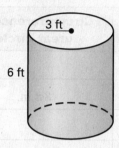
3 ft
6 ft
2 ft
4 ft

3.
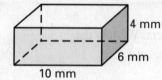
4 mm
6 mm
10 mm
4 mm
4 mm
5 mm

4.
2 m
3 m
4.5 m
1.2 m
1.8 m
2.7 m

5. Multiple Choice Which set of dimensions corresponds to a right cylinder that is similar to the cylinder shown?

A. $r = 2, h = 5$ **B.** $r = 3, h = 7$

C. $r = 10, h = 19$ **D.** $r = 15, h = 27$

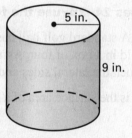
5 in.
9 in.

Solid A (shown) is similar to Solid B (not shown) with the given scale factor of A to B. Find the surface area and volume of Solid B.

6. Scale factor of $1:2$

$S = 42\pi$ ft^2, $V = 36\pi$ ft^3

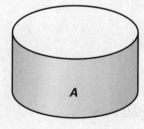
A

7. Scale factor of $1:3$

$S = 96\pi$ m^2, $V = 96\pi$ m^3

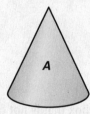
A

8. Scale factor of $2:3$

$S = 75.6$ cm^2, $V = 36$ cm^3

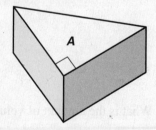
A

Name _____ Date _____

9. **Finding Surface Area** Two spheres have a scale factor of $1 : 3$. The smaller sphere has a surface area of 16π square feet. Find the surface area of the larger sphere.

10. **Multiple Choice** Two right cylinders are similar. The surface areas are 24π and 96π. What is the ratio of the volumes of the cylinders?

   A. $\dfrac{1}{4}$ **B.** $\dfrac{1}{8}$ **C.** $\dfrac{1}{2}$ **D.** $\dfrac{2}{3}$

Solid A is similar to Solid B. Find the scale factor of Solid A to Solid B.

11.
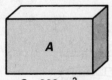

$S = 208$ m^2 $S = 52$ m^2

12.

$S = 63\pi$ cm^2 $S = 28\pi$ cm^2

13.
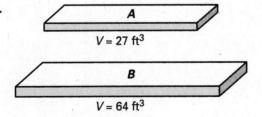
$V = 27$ ft^3

$V = 64$ ft^3

14.
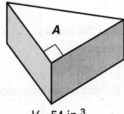
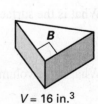
$V = 54$ in.^{3} $V = 16$ in.^{3}

<table><tr><td>LESSON
11.9</td><td>**Practice** *continued*
For use with the lesson "Explore Similar Solids"</td></tr></table>

Solid A is similar to Solid B. Find the surface area and volume of Solid B.

15.

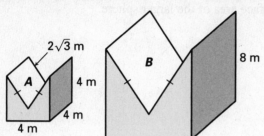

16.

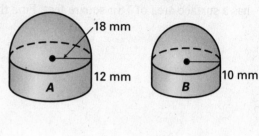

17. Finding a Ratio Two cubes have volumes of 64 cubic feet and 216 cubic feet. What is the ratio of the surface area of the smaller cube to the surface area of the larger cube?

In Exercises 18–22, use the following information.

Water Tower As part of a class project, you obtain the responsibility of making a scale model of the water tower in your town. The water tower's diameter is 12 feet and the height is 16 feet. You decide that 0.5 inch in your model will correspond to 12 inches of the actual water tower.

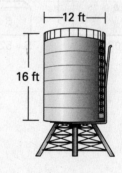

18. What is the scale factor?

19. What is the radius and height of the model?

20. What is the surface area of the model?

21. What is the volume of the actual water tower?

22. Use your result from Exercise 21 to find the volume of the model.

LESSON 12.1 Practice

For use with the lesson "Find Probabilities and Odds"

Find the number of possible outcomes in the sample space. Then list the possible outcomes.

1. A bag contains 6 blue cards numbered 1–6 and 8 red cards numbered 1–8. You choose a card at random.

2. You roll one 4-sided number cube and toss two coins.

3. You roll two 6-sided number cubes.

In Exercises 4–9, refer to the spinner shown. The spinner is divided into sections with the same area.

4. What is the probability that the spinner stops on an even number?

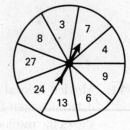

5. What is the probability that the spinner stops on an odd number?

6. You spin the spinner 24 times. It stops on 27 twice. What is the experimental probability of stopping on 27?

7. You spin the spinner 30 times. It stops on a multiple of 3 five times. What is the experimental probability of stopping on a multiple of 3?

8. What are the odds in favor of stopping on a multiple of 4?

9. What are the odds against stopping on a multiple of 6?

LESSON 12.1

Practice *continued*
For use with the lesson "Find Probabilities and Odds"

10. **Favorite Spectator Sport** A survey asked a total of 180 students in your school about their favorite spectator sports. The table shows the results of the survey.

Sport	Basketball	Soccer	Football	Baseball	Volleyball	Wrestling	Hockey
Number of students	40	20	45	20	16	18	21

a. What is the probability that a randomly selected student who participated in this survey chose football as his or her favorite spectator sport?

b. What is the probability that a randomly selected student who participated in this survey chose wrestling or hockey as his or her favorite spectator sport?

c. What are the odds in favor of a randomly selected student who participated in this survey choosing basketball as his or her favorite spectator sport?

11. **Movies** A local movie theater did a survey of students to determine their favorite types of movies. The circle graph shows the results of the survey.

    a. What is the probability that a randomly selected student chose science fiction as his or her favorite type of movie?

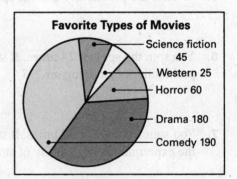

Favorite Types of Movies
- Science fiction 45
- Western 25
- Horror 60
- Drama 180
- Comedy 190

    b. What is the probability that a randomly selected student chose drama or comedy as his or her favorite type of movie?

LESSON 12.2 Practice

For use with the lesson "Find Probabilities Using Permutations"

Find the number of ways you can arrange (a) all of the letters in the given word and (b) 2 of the letters in the word.

1. TACK

2. MAR

3. GAMER

Write the meaning of the notation in words.

4. $_{14}P_3$

5. $_{24}P_{10}$

6. $_{30}P_{20}$

Evaluate the expression.

7. $6!$

8. $9!$

9. $11!$

10. $\dfrac{8!}{3!}$

11. $\dfrac{12!}{9!}$

12. $\dfrac{15!}{14!}$

13. $_6P_3$

14. $_4P_4$

15. $_{15}P_3$

16. $_8P_7$

17. $_{10}P_6$

18. $_5P_0$

LESSON 12.2 **Practice** *continued*
For use with the lesson "Find Probabilities Using Permutations"

Complete the statement using >, <, or =.

19. $_6P_4 \underline{\quad} {_4P_1}$

20. $_8P_6 \underline{\quad} {_{10}P_8}$

21. $_3P_0 \underline{\quad} {_6P_5}$

22. $_6P_3 \underline{\quad} {_4P_1}$

23. $_{24}P_1 \underline{\quad} {_4P_4}$

24. $_7P_5 \underline{\quad} {_{12}P_3}$

25. Summer Reading List At the beginning of the summer, you have 6 books to read. In how many orders can you read the books?

26. Air Conditioning Repair An air conditioner repair person has repairs to make at 7 different homes. The destinations are all so close, it doesn't matter the order in which the repairs are made. In how many orders can the repairs be made?

27. Boat Racing You are in a boat racing competition. In each heat, 4 boats race and the positions of the boats are randomly assigned.

   a. In how many ways can a position be assigned?

   b. What is the probability that you are chosen to be in the last position? *Explain* how you found your answer.

   c. What is the probability that you are chosen to be in the first or second position of the heat that you are racing in? *Explain* how you found your answer.

   d. What is the probability that you are chosen to be in the second or third position of the heat that you are racing in? *Compare* your answer with that in part (c).

28. Math Exam On an exam, you are asked to list the 6 steps to solving a particular kind of problem in order. You guess the order of the steps at random. What is the probability that you choose the correct order?

Practice
For use with the lesson "Find Probabilities Using Combinations"

Evaluate the expression.

1. $_8C_4$

2. $_5C_5$

3. $_{12}C_0$

4. $_7C_1$

5. $_{15}C_{11}$

6. $_{10}C_3$

7. $_6C_5$

8. $_4C_2$

9. $_{16}C_8$

Complete the statement using >, <, or =.

10. $_{10}C_6$ —— $_8C_5$

11. $_{22}C_3$ —— $_{18}C_4$

12. $_9C_6$ —— $_9C_3$

13. $_8C_2$ —— $_{15}C_{14}$

14. $_7C_7$ —— $_{14}C_{14}$

15. $_5C_3$ —— $_8C_3$

In Exercises 16–18, tell whether the question can be answered using
combinations **or** *permutations*. ***Explain*** **your choice, then answer**
the question.

16. Five students from the 90 students in your class not running for class president will
be selected to count the ballots for the vote for class president. In how many ways
can the 5 students be selected?

17. Twenty students are running for 3 different positions on student council. In how
many ways can the 3 positions be filled?

18. To complete a quiz, you must answer 3 questions from a list of 6 questions. In how
many ways can you complete the quiz?

LESSON 12.3

Practice *continued*
For use with the lesson "Find Probabilities Using Combinations"

19. Sweaters The buyer for a retail store must decide which sweaters to stock for the upcoming fall season. A sweater from one manufacturer comes in 5 different colors and 3 different textures. The buyer decides that the store will stock the sweater in 3 different colors and 2 different textures. How many different sweaters are possible?

20. Greeting Cards A greeting card company packages 4 different cards together that are randomly selected from 10 different cards with a different animal on each card. What is the probability that one of the cards in a package is the card that has a dog on it?

21. Open-Mike Night A coffee shop offers an open-mike night for poetry. Tonight, 15 people would like to read, but there is only enough time to have 7 people read.

   a. Seven of the 15 people that would like to read are randomly chosen. How many combinations of 7 readers from the group of people that would like to read are possible?

   b. You and your friend are part of the group that would like to read. What is the probability that you and your friend are chosen? What is the probability that you are chosen first and your friend is chosen second? Which event is more likely to occur?

LESSON
12.4

Practice
For use with the lesson "Find Probabilities of Disjoint and Overlapping Events"

Events A and B are disjoint. Find P(A or B).

1. $P(A) = 0.1, P(B) = 0.45$

2. $P(A) = 0.85, P(B) = 0.05$

3. $P(A) = \frac{1}{2}, P(B) = \frac{1}{5}$

Find the indicated probability.

4. $P(A) = \frac{1}{6}, P(B) = \frac{5}{6}$

$P(A \text{ or } B) = \frac{1}{3}$

$P(A \text{ and } B) = \underline{\quad ? \quad}$

5. $P(A) = 0.23, P(B) = 0.36$

$P(A \text{ or } B) = 0.25$

$P(A \text{ and } B) = \underline{\quad ? \quad}$

6. $P(A) = \frac{5}{8}, P(B) = \frac{1}{4}$

$P(A \text{ or } B) = \frac{1}{2}$

$P(A \text{ and } B) = \underline{\quad ? \quad}$

Find $P(\overline{A})$.

7. $P(A) = 1$

8. $P(A) = 0.25$

9. $P(A) = \frac{9}{16}$

Find the indicated probability. State whether A and B are disjoint events.

10. $P(A) = \frac{2}{13}, P(B) = \underline{\quad ? \quad}$

$P(A \text{ or } B) = \frac{8}{13}$

$P(A \text{ and } B) = \frac{4}{13}$

11. $P(A) = 17\%, P(B) = 35\%$

$P(A \text{ or } B) = 52\%$

$P(A \text{ and } B) = \underline{\quad ? \quad}$

12. $P(A) = \frac{5}{6}, P(B) = \frac{2}{5}$

$P(A \text{ or } B) = \underline{\quad ? \quad}$

$P(A \text{ and } B) = \frac{2}{3}$

LESSON 12.4 **Practice** *continued*
For use with the lesson *"Find Probabilities of Disjoint and Overlapping Events"*

Two six-sided dice are rolled. Find the probability of the given event. (Refer to Example 4 on page 709 of the textbook for the possible outcomes.)

13. The sum is greater than 4.

14. The sum is 6 or 11.

15. The sum is neither 5 nor 9.

16. The sum is greater than 7 and less than 11.

17. Honors Banquet Of the 120 students honored at an academic banquet, 40% won awards for mathematics and 55% for English. Fourteen of these students won awards for both mathematics and English. One of the 120 students is chosen at random to be interviewed for a newspaper article. What is the probability that the student won an award in mathematics or English?

18. Parakeets A pet store has 18 light green parakeets (5 females and 13 males) and 25 sky blue parakeets (15 females and 10 males). You randomly choose one of the parakeets. What is the probability that it is a male or a sky blue parakeet?

19. Potluck Dinner The organizer of a potluck dinner sends 6 people a list of 10 different recipes and asks each person to bring one of the items on the list. If all 6 people randomly choose a recipe from the list, what is the probability that at least 2 will bring the same thing?

LESSON 12.5 Practice

For use with the lesson "Find Probabilities of Independent and Dependent Events"

Tell whether the events are *independent* or *dependent*.

1. A shelf contains 50 travel books, one for each state. You randomly choose a book and put it back. Then you randomly choose another book.

   Event A: You choose the Alaska book first.

   Event B: You choose the Hawaii book second.

2. You have bottles of water and bottles of juice in your refrigerator. You randomly choose one, drink it, then randomly choose another.

   Event A: You choose a bottle of water first.

   Event B: You choose a bottle of juice second.

Events *A* and *B* are independent. Find the missing probability.

3. $P(A) = 0.6$
   $P(B) = 0.5$
   $P(A \text{ and } B) = \underline{\ ?\ }$

4. $P(A) = 0.35$
   $P(B) = \underline{\ ?\ }$
   $P(A \text{ and } B) = 0.28$

5. $P(A) = \underline{\ ?\ }$
   $P(B) = 0.8$
   $P(A \text{ and } B) = 0.24$

Events *A* and *B* are dependent. Find the missing probability.

6. $P(A) = 0.2$
   $P(B|A) = 0.3$
   $P(A \text{ and } B) = \underline{\ ?\ }$

7. $P(A) = 0.7$
   $P(B|A) = \underline{\ ?\ }$
   $P(A \text{ and } B) = 0.56$

8. $P(A) = \underline{\ ?\ }$
   $P(B|A) = 0.76$
   $P(A \text{ and } B) = 0.19$

LESSON
12.5
Practice continued
For use with the lesson "Find Probabilities of Independent and Dependent Events"

Find the probability of drawing the given cards from a standard deck of 52 cards (a) with replacement and (b) without replacement.

9. A red card, then a black card

10. A ten, then the ace of hearts

11. A face card, then a two

12. A club, then a four

HONORS CLASSES The table shows the number of students taking honors classes.

	1 Honors class	2 Honors classes	3 Honors classes
Freshmen	66	52	31
Sophomores	58	68	43
Juniors	51	72	60
Seniors	48	59	64

13. Find the probability that a student is a junior.

14. Find the probability that a sophomore who is taking honor classes is taking two honors classes.

15. Find the probability that a student taking two honors classes is a freshman.

16. **TIC-TAC-TOE** Woodrow wins a tic-tac-toe game 65% of the time when he chooses the first square and 32% of the time when his opponent chooses the first square. The player who plays first is chosen by a coin toss. What is the probability that Woodrow wins a given game?